Light the Fire

Fiery Food with a Light New Attitude!

by Linda Matthie-Jacobs

Fiery Food with a Light New Attitude!

by Linda Matthie-Jacobs

Published by: The MJM Grande Publishing Company Ltd.
Box 4031, Station C
Calgary, Alberta, Canada T2T 5M9
Phone: 1-888-MJM-FIRE
E-mail: mjmgrand@cadvision.com
Website: http://www.cookingwithfire.com

Canadian Cataloging in Publication Data

Matthie-Jacobs, Linda, 1959-

Light the fire

Includes index.
ISBN 1-894202-55-4

1. Cookery (Hot peppers). 2. Low fat diet – Recipes.
I. Title.

TX819.H66M388 1998 641.6'384 C98-920108-2

Photography by: Richard Warren,
R.G.W. Commercially Focused Photography, Red Deer, Alberta

Photo Design and Propping by:
Barry Weiss, Barry Weiss Intuitive Design, Calgary, Alberta

Food Styling by:
Natalie Schnell, B.Sc. (H.Ec.), R.D., Red Deer, Alberta

Cover and Page Design by:
Jennifer Nelson, The Big Picture, Red Deer, Alberta

Printed in Canada by: Centax Books,
a division of PrintWest Communications Ltd.,
1150 Eighth Avenue Regina, Saskatchewan S4R 1C9
(306) 525-2304 FAX: (306) 757-2439

Table of Contents

Recipes have been tested in U.S. Standard measurements. Common metric measurements are given as a convenience for those who are more familiar with metric. Recipes have not been tested in metric.

The Oxford dictionary defines fire as "combustion producing light and heat". The global warming trend that we continue to hear about is not just an environmental issue but describes the hottest movement in food pursuits. Combined with a growing concern and focus to lower fat and reduce salt, I've written this book to share my burning desire for the healthy, fiery foods of the world.

This book features an eclectic collection of recipes with a decidedly strong spirit of Mexican and southwestern flavors (simply because that is the cuisine my husband and I have been most exposed to in our travels), but introduces other fiery flavors of the world as well. Interestingly, some of the "hottest" cuisines of the world originate in countries with consistently warm climates. From the sizzling salsas of Mexico, to the jarring jerk of the Caribbean, to the tongue-tingling food from India, these cuisines all share a common passion for "heat".

I cook with a conscious focus on creating food that celebrates flavor and fun and, in most recipes, I attempt to keep the fat content low without sacrificing flavor. Although I usually prepare foods that are salt-free and low in fat, we occasionally indulge in a decadent dessert or a dish that isn't low in fat or calories. Our society has developed tremendous fear and guilt over these occasional indulgences, but I believe that most things are fine in moderation. Food should be enjoyed and a balanced lifestyle, including exercise, is the key.

This book will lead you through a full range of menu categories and promises to deliver a spicy and innovative array of sizzling and satisfying recipes. The food will thrill your palate and will extinguish your desire for unnecessary fats, oils and salt. I've intentionally excluded salt from the recipes, as I believe that the flavors of the foods are enhanced sufficiently with the ingredients themselves. I've created these recipes for people who enjoy hot and healthy food and whose lives are as busy as mine (I have a full-time career in the petroleum industry in addition to our publishing business). I don't claim to be a food expert. I do, however, develop recipes and write for people, like me, who love fabulous food and entertaining friends and family. The recipes are easy-to-follow and focus on the needs and interests of contemporary cooks, from beginner to experienced, with busy lifestyles.

Most of the ingredients used in the recipes are readily available in most supermarkets and larger grocery stores, with the exception of red, green and chipotle chile powders that we've made available to you via mail order (see information at the back of the book or check out our website located at http://www.cookingwithfire.com). These spices are organically grown, packaged and labeled in New Mexico under our "Cooking with Fire" private label and offer a truly unique taste experience.

I hope this exciting collection of recipes sets your taste buds tingling and brings you rich memories of joy-filled times of sharing fabulous food with family and friends. Experience fiery foods in a whole new "light" and satisfy the eternal quest for "fire" with "Light the Fire – Fiery Food with a Light New Attitude!"

¡Salud! (Cheers!)

Linda

This book is dedicated
to the memory of our beloved Bran.

Acknowledgements

This book is the result of the tremendous collaboration and support of some incredible people that I cherish deeply.

First, foremost and forever, I'd like to express my eternal gratitude to my husband, Jim, for his endless love and support. He is my soulmate, my best friend and he inspires the passion that drives my life everyday. He is the most patient partner, the most willing recipe taster and the best business manager in the world. Muchisimas gracias, me amor - eres toda mi vida.

I'd like to send sincere thanks to my parents, Elsie and Carl Matthie, for their eternal love, guidance, support and encouragement. Thank you for all the love you've given us - we love you more than we can ever express, forever and always.

On the back cover, you'll notice that there is a photograph of a very special group of people. It was absolutely critical to me that they be on the back cover beside me. Although you aren't able to clearly make out the individuals, this book wouldn't have been possible without them and I am indescribably grateful to each and every one of them. Let me introduce them as they appear in the photo, starting from the left and moving clockwise:

- Barry Weiss (Barry Weiss Intuitive Design of Calgary) is a brilliant artist who is responsible for creating the concepts and design of each incredible photo in the book and was unbelievably inventive in locating props (thanks again to James, Shelagh and my parents!). I'm so grateful for Barry's artistry, but even more grateful for Barry's friendship, which has grown deeply since we worked on The "Fire 'n' Ice Cookbook" together.

- The love of my life, Jim.

- Natalie Schnell (of Red Deer), who was introduced to this project by Richard Warren. Natalie is not only an incredibly talented food stylist and authority on food, but one of the warmest and most wonderful people you could ever meet. Thank you for making the food look so good and for making the week shooting in Red Deer so much fun, Nat!

- Richard Warren (R.G.W. Commercially Focused Photography of Red Deer) is a long-time and valued friend. Richard is responsible for the stunning photographs in both "Light the Fire" and in "The Fire 'n' Ice Cookbook". Richard possesses profound artistic and technical talent and his eye for detail and light is unsurpassed. Your work is brilliant, Richard - thank you!

- Debbie Black (Debco Creative Solutions of Calgary) is a publicist extraordinaire as well as a dear and cherished friend. Your sensitivity, creative talent, boundless energy and fabulous sense of humor add so much joy to our lives. You give so much of yourself, Deb, and we sincerely appreciate everything. The most remarkable work means nothing if no one knows about it - thank you so much for all that you do and for being the incredible friend that you are!

- Jennifer Nelson (The Big Picture of Red Deer) is responsible for the exquisite cover and original page design of this book as well as for "The Fire 'n' Ice Cookbook". Jennifer is incredibly talented and has a vision of what makes a book both beautiful and functional. Thank you for making people pick up this book with your beautiful design, but most of all, Jen, for your friendship.

The most rewarding things that have resulted from the writing "Light the Fire", co-authoring "The Fire 'n' Ice Cookbook" and running this publishing business, have been the incredible people I've met along the way and the experiences that have made my life so much richer.

I'd like to sincerely thank Sheri Morrish, co-author of "The Fire 'n' Ice Cookbook", for sharing the first five years in this business with me. Sheri started writing this book with me (and has contributed some of the recipes), but decided to leave the business to pursue other interests. We shared some great times and experiences together and I'm eternally grateful that we were able to start this journey as business partners. I think of you often and miss you a great deal.

I'd like to express sincere gratitude to Margo Embury and Iona Glabus of Centax Books. Margo's incredible talent as an editor, writer and food specialist is unsurpassed. She is a consummate professional and a true pleasure to work with. Iona made innumerable changes to the manuscript and her patience and accuracy are greatly appreciated.

My heartfelt thanks to family, friends and colleagues for their encouragement, enthusiasm and support of this journey and the attainment of a dream.

Last, but certainly not least, thanks to all those people who share a passion for "fiery food with a light new attitude".

¡Salud! (Cheers!)

I thought it might be helpful to put together some menu suggestions. So often we flip through a book like this and, until we've tried all the recipes, we aren't sure which recipes to combine to create that special menu. Here are a few suggestions that will make your use of this book more enjoyable and will fire up your enthusiasm for fiery foods with a light new attitude:

Summer Brunch on the Deck

Watermelon Margaritas (page 26)

Lemon Ginger Scones (page 40)

Banana Bran Muffins with a Bite (page 42)

Green Chile Honey (page 155)

Margarita Fruit Salad (page 14)

Cornmeal Pancakes with Serrano and Ginger (page 19)

Winter Brunch

Rattlesnake Bite (page 24)

Cheesy Chile Corn Muffins (page 44)

Spicy Hash Browns (page 15)

Green Chile Frittata (page 16)

Barbecue Dinner

Refreshing Iced Mint Tea (page 32)

Grilled Quesadillas (page 50)

Tangy Tomato Salad (page 70)

Marinated Sirloin Steaks (page 120)

Grilled Marinated Vegetables (page 122)

Corn on the Cob (page 138)

Grilled Fruit Kebabs (page 172)

Spring Dinner Party

Tequila Mockingbird (page 29)
Jícama with Lime and Red Chile (page 59)
Fiery Chilled Soup (page 85)
Grilled Tequila Salmon Steaks (page 110)
Risotto with Roasted Vegetables (page 146)
Green Beans with Dill and Pine Nuts (page 135)
Jenny's Pavlova (page 181)

Warm Winter Dinner Party

Sangrita (page 25)
Garlic and Cheese Stuffed Mushrooms (page 63)
Black Bean Soup (page 94)
Jalapeño Pepper Jelly Glazed Chicken Breasts (page 114)
Arroz Rojo (page 142)
Stuffed Poblano Chiles (page 131)
Apple, Cranberry and Red Chile Crisp (page 184)

Vegetarian Dinner

Baked Brie with Roasted Garlic (page 64)
Bueno Broccoli Salad (page 68)
Vegetarian Chili (page 102)
Pan Roasted Chipotle Corn Bread (page 45)
Salsa Cream Cheese (page 48)
Cantaloupe Dessert Soup (page 170)

Mexican Dinner

Tartas con Chorizo (page 55)

Sopa de Lima (page 93)

Chili Verde Burritos (page 117)

Chile and Potato Gratin (page 136)

Mexican Vegetable Medley (page 124)

Decadent Strawberry Nachos (page 174)

East Indian Dinner

Chicken and Vegetable Curry (page 116)

Madras Vegetables (page 127)

Saffron Rice with Toasted Pine Nuts (page 141)

Tomato Chutney (page 152)

Sherried Pine Nut Yogurt (page 178)

Caribbean Dinner

Caribbean Sea Breeze (page 27)

Roasted Red Pepper Soup (page 87)

Jamaican Jerk Chicken (page 115)

Raging Red Beans and Rice (page 145)

Grilled Marinated Vegetables (page 122)

Caramel Banana Tortillas (page 175)

Elegant Dinner Party

Artichoke and Feta Cheese Roll with Roasted Red Pepper Sauce (page 56)

Mixed Greens with Piquant Vinaigrette (page 69)

Chilled Beet Soup with Spicy Cilantro Pesto (page 84)

Pasta Azteca (page 106)

Mexican Chocolate Truffle Tart with Sinful Sauce (page 176)

Everyday Meals

Tempting Two-Pepper Biscuits (page 41)

Great Bowls of Fire (page 101)

Green Chile Chocolate Chip Cookies (page 182)

Pesto Pizza (page 103)

La Fresa Sorpresa (page 171)

Southwestern Cheese Toast (page 57)

Southwestern Grilled Chicken Caesar Salad (page 80)

Lime Liquado with Mint (page 34)

Cocktail Party

Tequila Crantinis (page 29)

Firewater (page 30)

Black Bean Roll-Ups (page 51)

Chili con Queso (page 62)

Roasted Red Pepper Hummus (page 61)

Tortilla Torte (page 52)

Charred Pico de Gallo (page 151)

Baked Artichoke-Parmesan Dip (page 65)

Come for Dessert and Coffee

Mayan Iced Coffee (page 33)

Chile-Cherry Bread Pudding with Cherry Sauce (page 183)

Afternoon Delight

Mexican Hot Chocolate (page 38)

Pumpkin Bread with Cranberries (page 47)

Cranberry-Orange Cream Cheese (page 48)

Hockey or Football Party

Tequila Slush (page 28)

Santa Fe Snack Mix (page 66)

Popcorn with Savory Popcorn Seasoning (page 164)

Great Gifts

Firewater (page 30)

Santa Fe Snack Mix (page 66)

Margarita Jelly (page 156)

Sweet Heat (page 159)

Savory Popcorn Seasoning (page 164)

Spicy Cornmeal Crisps (page 163)

Chocolate Chile Pretzels (page 165)

Green Chile Honey (page 155)

Oil of Olé (page 154)

Spicy Chile Vinegar (page 155)

Radiant Rub (page 166)

Brunch Dishes

Grilled Vegetable Sandwiches

Fabulous with a tossed green salad for a major brunch hit!

Herbed Balsamic Marinade:

2	tbsp.	olive oil	30	mL
1/4	cup	balsamic vinegar	60	mL
2	tsp.	molasses	10	mL
1	tsp.	dried basil	5	mL
1/2	tsp.	dried thyme	2	mL
1/4	tsp.	black pepper	1	mL

1		large onion, cut into 1/2" (1.3 cm) slices	1	
3		medium zucchini, cut lengthwise into 1/4" (1 cm) thick oblong slices	3	
1	each	medium yellow, orange, red bell pepper, cut into 6 wedges	1	
1		large loaf French bread	1	
1/2	cup	crumbled, seasoned feta cheese (tomato and basil, herb and garlic, etc.)	125	mL
2	tbsp.	fat-free mayonnaise	30	mL
1/4	cup	grated Parmesan cheese	60	mL

Combine marinade ingredients in a large heavy-duty zip-top plastic bag. Add vegetables and seal bag. Marinate in the refrigerator for at least 2 hours to allow flavors to permeate and blend, turning bag occasionally. Remove vegetables from the bag. Reserve marinade.

Cut French bread loaf in half horizontally. Using a pastry brush, brush 2 tbsp. (30 mL) of reserved marinade over each half of bread. Set bread and remaining marinade aside.

Preheat grill and coat wire grilling basket or grilling wok with nonstick cooking spray. Place vegetables in grilling basket or wok and cook on the grill for 10 minutes, basting occasionally with remaining marinade and turning frequently.

When vegetables are close to being cooked tender-crisp and browned on all sides, place bread, cut sides down, on grill and cook for 3 minutes, or until toasted.

In a small bowl, combine feta and mayonnaise; stir well. Spread mayonnaise mixture over both toasted sides of French bread. Place grilled vegetables on bottom half of loaf and sprinkle with Parmesan cheese. Replace top half of bread. Cut loaf diagonally into 6 pieces.

Serves 6.

Margarita Fruit Salad

Tequila Orange Liqueur Dressing:

3	tbsp.	tequila	45	mL
3	tbsp.	orange-flavored liqueur (Triple Sec, Cointreau or Grand Marnier)	45	mL
3	tbsp.	orange marmalade	45	mL
1		lime, juice of, 1-2 tbsp. (15-30 mL)	1	

Fruit Salad:

4	cups	sliced strawberries	1	L
4		oranges, peeled, sectioned and cut in small pieces	4	
1		small honeydew melon, rind and seeds removed and cut in small pieces	1	
1		small cantaloupe melon, rind and seeds removed and cut in small pieces	1	

In a large bowl, mix together tequila, orange-flavored liqueur, orange marmalade and lime juice. Add strawberries, oranges, honeydew and cantaloupe. Stir to combine and refrigerate for several hours or overnight to allow the flavors to blend.

Serves 6.

Spicy Hash Browns

A quick and tasty side dish to serve at a weekend brunch.

2	tbsp.	olive oil	30	mL
1	tsp.	paprika	5	mL
1	tsp.	red chile powder	5	mL
1/4	tsp.	cayenne pepper	1	mL
1/4	tsp.	black pepper	1	mL
6		medium baking potatoes, diced	6	

Preheat oven to 400°F (200°C).

In a large heavy-duty zip-top plastic bag, add first 5 ingredients and massage to mix well. Add potatoes and massage well to coat. Place potatoes in a single layer on a baking sheet coated with nonstick cooking spray.

Bake for 30 minutes, or until evenly browned.

Serves 6.

Pictured on page 17.

Green Chile Frittata

This lighter version of a classic Italian omelet has the added fire of chile powder and jalapeños.

½	cup	thinly sliced green onions	125	mL
4	oz	can diced green chiles, drained	114	g
2	tsp.	green chile powder	10	mL
1	tsp.	ground cumin	5	mL
8		large egg whites, lightly beaten	8	
2		large egg yolks, lightly beaten	2	
4		garlic cloves, minced	4	
½	cup	shredded Monterey Jack cheese	125	mL
1	tsp.	finely chopped pickled jalapeño peppers	5	mL
4	tbsp.	fat-free sour cream, for garnish	60	mL
4	tbsp.	salsa, for garnish	60	mL
4		cilantro sprigs, for garnish	4	

Preheat oven to 450°F (230°C).

Combine onions, green chiles, chile powder, cumin, egg whites and egg yolks; stir well. Set aside.

Coat a large nonstick, ovenproof skillet with nonstick cooking spray and place over medium heat until hot. Add garlic and sauté until garlic becomes very fragrant but not browned, about 1 minute. Lower heat to medium-low and pour in egg mixture. Cook for about 5 minutes, or until eggs are almost set.

Place skillet in oven and bake for 5 minutes, or until fully set. Sprinkle cheese over frittata and bake for an additional minute, or until cheese melts.

Cut frittata into 4 wedges and place individual portions on plates. Top each serving with a tablespoon (15 mL) of sour cream and a tablespoon (15 mL) of salsa. Garnish with cilantro sprigs.

Serves 4.

Pictured on opposite page.

Brunch Dishes

Clockwise from front lefthand side:

Green Chile Frittata, page 16
Cheesy Chile Corn Muffins, page 44
Rattlesnake Bite, page 24
Spicy Hash Browns, page 15

Cornmeal Pancakes with Serrano and Ginger

You'll never think pancakes are boring fare again!

1	cup	cornmeal	250	mL
1	cup	flour	250	mL
2	tbsp.	sugar	30	mL
1	tbsp.	baking powder	15	mL
½	tsp.	baking soda	2	mL
2		eggs, lightly beaten	2	
1¼	cups	low-fat milk	310	mL
2	tbsp.	vegetable oil	30	mL
1		serrano or jalapeño pepper, finely chopped	1	
2	tbsp.	grated fresh ginger root	30	mL

Preheat oven to 200°F (93°C).

In a large bowl, combine cornmeal, flour, sugar, baking powder and baking soda.

In a medium bowl, combine eggs, milk, oil, serrano and ginger. Pour into dry ingredients and mix until just combined.

Spray nonstick skillet with nonstick cooking spray. Heat skillet over medium heat and spoon in batter for each pancake. Cook until the surface bubbles and the underside is golden brown. Turn and cook until bottom is golden brown as well.

Place cooked pancakes in covered casserole and keep warm in oven until all pancakes are cooked and ready to serve.

Serves 6 (3 pancakes each).

Serrano Peppers

Serrano peppers are bright green and turn orange and then yellow as they mature. Smaller and hotter than jalapeños, they are available fresh, pickled or canned.

Southwestern Vegetable Pies

Red Chile Cornmeal Crust:

1/2	cup	flour	125	mL
1/2	cup	cornmeal	125	mL
2	tsp.	red chile powder	10	mL
1	cup	milk	250	mL
4		eggs, lightly beaten	4	

Southwestern Pie Filling:

1	tsp.	vegetable oil	5	mL
6		green onions, thinly sliced	6	
1/2		medium green bell pepper, chopped	1/2	
1/2		medium red bell pepper, chopped	1/2	
1/2		medium yellow bell pepper, chopped	1/2	
2		garlic cloves, minced	2	
12	oz.	can kernel corn, drained	341	mL
1/2	cup	salsa	125	mL
1/2	tsp.	coriander	2	mL
1/2	tsp.	cumin	2	mL
1/2	tsp.	oregano	2	mL
2	tbsp.	lime juice	30	mL
2x14	oz.	cans pinto beans, drained and rinsed	2x390	mL
2		medium tomatoes, chopped	2	
1	cup	shredded light Cheddar cheese	250	mL
		fat-free sour cream, for garnish		
		parsley sprigs		

Preheat oven to 475°F (240°C).

In a medium bowl, combine flour, cornmeal and chile powder. Gradually add milk and eggs, while stirring with a whisk, until well combined.

Divide the crust mixture between two, 9" (23 cm) pie plates that have been coated with nonstick cooking spray. Spread crust mixture into pie plates and press gently to form crusts. Bake for 10 minutes, or until puffed and browned.

Meanwhile, heat oil in a large nonstick skillet over medium-high heat. Add green onions, peppers and garlic, and sauté for 3 minutes, or until vegetables are tender.

Stir in corn, salsa, seasonings, lime juice, beans and tomatoes. Cook until heated through, about 10 to 15 minutes.

Divide the vegetable mixture between the 2 pies, and sprinkle each with half of the cheese. Bake just until the cheese melts, about 1 minute.

Remove from oven and let set for 5 minutes. Cut each pie into 6 pieces and serve immediately. Garnish each piece with a spoonful of fat-free sour cream and a parsley sprig.

Serves 6 (2 slices each).

Vegetable Oil

I generally use canola oil in recipes that call for "vegetable" oil because it is lower in saturated fat, which tends to raise blood cholesterol, than any other oil. It also has more monounsaturated fat, which balances cholesterol, than any oil except for olive oil. Canola oil contains Omega 3 fatty acids, which are said to lower cholesterol and triglycerides and also contribute to brain development and growth. It has very little flavor, which allows the flavor of the other ingredients to dominate. (I'm also a little partial because my family used to grow the canola seed that the oil is made from.) Canola oil has a very high smoking point, which is necessary for oils used for frying or sautéing. Beware of most "light" vegetable oils as they are generally only light in color and flavor, not in fat and calories. You don't need to use much canola oil when using a high-quality oil for cooking.

Breakfast Bake with a Bite

This is a great make-ahead brunch dish when you a have a house full of company and want to serve something simple and delicious.

1	cup	shredded light Cheddar cheese	250	mL
1	cup	shredded light Monterey Jack cheese	250	mL
1	cup	chopped green onion	250	mL
2		jalapeño peppers, finely chopped	2	
5		egg whites	5	
1		egg	1	
2½	cups	skim milk	625	mL
2x4	oz	cans diced green chiles, drained	2x114	g
3		garlic cloves, minced	3	
1	tsp.	dry mustard	5	mL
1	tsp.	red chile powder	5	mL
½	tsp.	cayenne pepper	2	mL
¼	tsp.	black pepper	1	mL
1	tsp.	Worcestershire sauce	5	mL
½	tsp.	hot pepper sauce	2	mL
8	cups	cubed Italian or French bread	2	L
1		medium red bell pepper	1	
3		green onions, chopped	3	
½	cup	shredded light Cheddar cheese	125	mL

In a medium bowl, combine cheeses, green onion and jalapeño pepper. Set aside.

In a large bowl, whisk together eggs, milk, green chiles, garlic, dry mustard, red chile, cayenne pepper, black pepper, Worcestershire sauce and hot pepper sauce.

Arrange half of the bread cubes in a 9 x 13" (23 x 33 cm) baking dish that has been coated with nonstick cooking spray. Top with half of the cheese mixture. Repeat layers and pour egg mixture over top. Cover with plastic wrap and refrigerate for at least 8 hours or for up to 24 hours.

When ready to cook, preheat oven to 350°F (180°C). Core and seed red pepper and cut crosswise into thin rings. Arrange on top and sprinkle with chopped green onions. Sprinkle with ½ cup (125 mL) of shredded Cheddar cheese. Bake, uncovered, for 60 minutes, or until golden brown and a knife inserted in center comes out clean. Serve immediately.

Serves 6.

BEVERAGES

Rattlesnake Bite

4	cups	pineapple juice	1	L
1/2	cup	tomato juice	125	mL
1	tbsp.	powdered sugar	15	mL
1	tsp.	hot pepper sauce	5	mL
1		lime, juice of		
3/4	cup	vodka	175	mL
		ice cubes		
		lime slices, for garnish		

In a glass pitcher, combine pineapple juice, tomato juice, powdered sugar, hot pepper sauce, lime juice and vodka. Stir to mix well.

Serve over ice and garnish with lime slices.

Serves 6.

Pictured on page 17.

Hot Sauces are Hot!

Hot sauces have taken the market by storm! There are well over 1000 different hot sauces on the market and some people collect them like others collect stamps. The lure of the perfect blend is what motivates most hot sauce creators, with a conscious focus on flavor. There are basically three different styles of hot sauce:

Louisiana Style – The sauces are traditionally a blend of fermented cayenne or tabasco pepper mash, vinegar and salt, although new versions are appearing which add or substitute different ingredients to this style of sauce;

Caribbean Style – Sauces in this style are traditionally a combination of fruits, curries and peppers – usually the habañero pepper (the pepper with the highest heat rating of all!);

Mexican Style – These sauces usually highlight a specific pepper, such as serrano, jalapeño or chipotle, and often use a tomato base.

Hot sauces are excellent in sauces and stir-frys, make quick and handy marinades before grilling food, and are always welcome condiments on the table.

Sangrita

This drink makes me think of sitting in the jacuzzi at Ocho Cascadas in Puerto Vallarta with Jim. ¡Muy deliciouso y muy romantico!

2	cups	tomato juice	500	mL
2	cups	orange juice	500	mL
1	cup	tequila	250	mL
2	tbsp	grenadine	30	mL
2	tsp	Worcestershire sauce	10	mL
2	tsp	Tabasco sauce	10	mL
		black pepper, to taste		
		orange slices, for garnish		

In a glass pitcher, combine all ingredients except pepper and orange slices.

Pour juice mixture over ice into each of 6 glasses. Season with pepper and garnish with an orange slice.

Serves 6.

Tabasco Sauce History

Tabasco sauce has become a staple ingredient in many kitchens and diets over the years (where would a Caesar or Bloody Mary be without it!). The McIlhenny family of Avery Island, Louisiana has been producing their famous Tabasco sauce since 1868. This original sauce contains only Tabasco peppers, vinegar and salt, fermented naturally in wood for three years, and remains a classic among its many competitors. In addition to the original Tabasco, the McIlhenny family expanded their line with the introduction of gift ware, a jalapeño pepper sauce and have most recently brought out a habañero sauce. An incredible family success story!

Watermelon Margaritas

2	tsp.	sugar	10	mL
2		fresh limes, cut in half	2	
4	cups	seedless watermelon, cut in 2" (5 cm) chunks	1	L
2	tbsp.	sugar	30	mL
½	cup	tequila	125	mL
¼	cup	orange-flavored liqueur (Triple Sec, Cointreau or Grand Marnier)	60	mL
		lime wedges, for garnish		
		watermelon balls, for garnish		

Place 2 tsp. (10 mL) sugar in a small dish. Rub rim of margarita glasses with 1 cut half of lime, and then roll glasses in sugar to coat. Place prepared glasses in the freezer until ready to serve drinks.

Combine juice of limes, watermelon, 2 tbsp. (30 mL) sugar, tequila and orange-flavored liqueur in a blender and process until smooth. Fill blender with ice cubes and process until mixture is a slush consistency. Fill prepared glasses with margaritas, garnish each glass with a lime wedge and watermelon balls on a skewer (see photograph on page 35) and serve immediately.

Serves 6.

Pictured on page 35.

With fiery foods or on a hot summer day it's hard to beat the refreshing coolness of watermelon. Native to Africa, watermelons can vary in color from yellow to white, pink and the familiar luscious red. When you slap a ripe watermelon, you hear a hollow-sounding thunk. Use cut watermelon within 1 to 2 days, and store in the refrigerator. The seeds can be roasted and the rind pickled. Watermelons contain fair amounts of Vitamins A and C.

Caribbean Sea Breeze

Jim and I have had the great pleasure of visiting the Caribbean several times over the years and this drink takes us back to those beautiful emerald seas, the incredible beauty of the islands and the many fabulous people we've had the pleasure to meet.

3	oz.	spiced rum (such as Bacardi)	90	mL
1	oz.	cranberry juice	30	mL
1	oz.	fresh orange juice	30	mL
1	oz.	fresh lime juice	30	mL
		ice		
2		lime twists, for garnish	2	

Pour rum, cranberry juice, orange juice and lime juice over ice in a cocktail shaker. Shake well. Strain and serve in martini glasses and garnish each glass with a lime twist.

Serves 2.

Rum

The Caribbean's gift to the world, rums from various parts of the Caribbean have distinctive colors and flavors. White or silver rum from Puerto Rico is light and clear. Amber and golden rums, also from Puerto Rico have a slightly deeper color and flavor. Jamaican and Cuban rums are rich, dark and full bodied. Demerara rum from Guyana is the strongest, darkest and richest in flavor. Rum goes well with fresh fruit and fruit juices in drinks and desserts.

Tequila Slush

Otherwise known as the official family "fire extinguisher"!

2x12½	oz.	cans frozen limeade, thawed	2x355	mL
12½	oz.	can frozen orange juice, thawed	355	mL
12½	oz.	can tequila	355	mL
½x12½	oz.	can orange-flavored liqueur (Triple Sec, Cointreau or Grand Marnier)	178	ml
6x12½	oz.	cans water	2.25	L
8	cups	Sprite, Squirt or other lemon-lime flavored soda	2	L

After the cans of limeade and orange juice have been emptied, use the empty cans to measure the tequila, orange-flavored liqueur and water. Mix all ingredients in a large plastic container and freeze.

Remove from freezer 30 minutes before serving and stir with a spoon until slushy. Scoop slush into glasses and garnish with slices of lime or orange.

Slush can be refrozen and kept indefinitely.

Serves lots!

Tequila

Originally from Tequila, Mexico, tequila is made from the sap of the agave plant. It is colorless or slightly golden and is used in margaritas and other fruit-based cocktails. Tequila can range in strength from 80 to over 100 proof.

Tequila Crantinis

These are unbelievably smooth – be careful!

2	oz.	tequila, preferably an ultra-smooth brand such as Cuervo 1800 or Patrón Silver	60	mL
1/2	oz.	orange-flavored liqueur, (Triple Sec, Cointreau or Grand Marnier)	15	mL
1/2	cup	cranberry juice	125	mL
		ice		
6		frozen cranberries	6	

Pour tequila, orange-flavored liqueur and cranberry juice over ice in a cocktail shaker. Shake well. Strain and serve in chilled martini glasses. Garnish with 3 frozen cranberries per glass.

Serves 2.

Tequila Mockingbird

1/2	cup	unsweetened apple cider	125	mL
2	oz.	tequila	60	mL
1	oz.	black currant-flavored liqueur (such as Cassis)	30	mL
2	tsp.	fresh lime juice	10	mL
		ice		

Pour apple cider, tequila, black currant-flavored liqueur and lime juice over ice in a cocktail shaker. Shake well. Pour contents of cocktail shaker, including ice, into 2 old-fashioned glasses and enjoy!

Serves 2.

Firewater

In Russian, vodka literally means "little water". Vodka, like water, is easy to infuse with a host of flavors and colors. Jim and I were first introduced to "firewater" many years ago in Puerto Vallarta and we present our version of this fiery sipping drink that blends the fire of chiles with some Russian "water".

1		pasilla chile, stems and seeds removed, cut into small pieces	1	
1/4		habañero chile, stem and seeds removed, left intact	1/4	
40	oz.	bottle of vodka, preferably an ultra-smooth brand	1.25	L

Place chiles in the vodka; replace cap, and allow to steep for 1 week. The vodka will get progressively hotter the longer it is allowed to sit, but you can add fresh vodka to replace the firewater as you drink it.

Before serving, strain the infused vodka to remove any solids. Serve over ice in a martini glass. Or, for a more dramatic presentation, refrigerate firewater, strain and serve in a martini glass with a whole serrano or jalapeño pepper in the bottom.

Serves lots!

Pasilla Chiles

The pasilla chile, otherwise known as chile negro, is a dried chilaca chile, brownish-black in color, long (about 6" [15 cm] in length by 1" [2.5 cm] wide), tapered and wrinkled. The name "pasilla" translates as "little raisin" and they have a wonderfully dark and rich, hot flavor.

Next time you're sick with a cold or the flu, try this recipe that has a decongestant effect on sinus and bronchial congestion. It sounds terrible, but the combined flavors are surprisingly good and the capsaicin really clears the congestion and speeds up the metabolism.

2	tbsp.	maple syrup	30	mL
2	tbsp.	lemon juice, freshly squeezed	30	mL
	dash	cayenne pepper		dash
3/4	cup	boiling water	175	mL

Take a large coffee mug and measure in the maple syrup and lemon juice. Add a healthy dash of cayenne pepper and fill mug with boiling water. Stir, drink while hot and enjoy being able to breathe again! By the way, when you're sick, this will always taste better when someone else makes it for you!

Serves 1 sick person.

Capsaicin – Medicinal Uses

Capsaicin, a chemical found in hot peppers, has been used medicinally for centuries. Hot peppers were one of the first plants domesticated in the Americas. Archaeologists believe people in Mexico were eating chiles and peppers as early as 7000 BC. Ancient pain-relievers and other medications used capsaicin as a major ingredient.

Capsaicin has been proven to be highly successful in relieving symptoms of arthritis, sports injuries, other kinds of chronic joint and muscle pain, and certain kinds of itching. Capsaicin cream was originally used to treat the intense pain of herpes zoster (shingles), which is a nerve infection caused by chicken pox and usually afflicts adults. Medical studies have shown that Capsaicin significantly lowers cholesterol levels and is a factor in warding off strokes and heart attacks.

Refreshing Iced Mint Tea

Something cool and refreshing to offset the fire!

4		tea bags	4	
10		sprigs fresh mint	10	
5	cups	boiling water	1.25	L
1	cup	sugar	250	mL
3	cups	boiling water	750	mL
2/3	cup	fresh lemon juice	150	mL
1/3	cup	fresh orange juice	75	mL

Put tea bags, mint and 5 cups (1.25 L) of boiling water in a large covered container. Let sit for 30 minutes.

Mix sugar and 3 cups (750 mL) boiling water in a smaller container and stir until sugar is dissolved. Add lemon and orange juices.

Remove tea bags and add sugar and juice mixture to tea mixture. Stir to combine. Refrigerate until ready to drink. Strain and serve over ice.

Serves 10.

Iced Tea Origins

In 1904, at the St. Louis World's Fair, the sweltering heat made Englishman Richard Blechynden's hot tea booth less than popular. He changed that by adding ice, lemon and sweeteners to his hot brew. Iced tea can be made with black teas or with the wide variety of fruit and herbal teas now available. Brew tea double strength, pour over ice and add lemon, mint, honey or sugar and even rum if you wish.

Mayan Iced Coffee

A perfect pick-me-up on a hot summer day.

4	tsp.	instant coffee granules (espresso granules, if available)	20	mL
2	tsp.	sugar	10	mL
2	tbsp.	boiling water	30	mL
2	cups	skim milk	500	mL
		ice		
		instant coffee granules, for garnish		

Combine instant coffee, sugar and boiling water in a beverage container with a tight-fitting lid. Stir until instant coffee granules and sugar are dissolved. Add milk and shake vigorously until well combined. Pour into tall glasses over ice and garnish with a sprinkle of instant coffee granules.

Serves 2.

Coffee

Brazil and Columbia produce the largest amount of coffee although coffee plantations are found throughout South America, Central America, Hawaii, Cuba, Jamaica, Indonesia and many African countries, including Ethiopia where coffee beans originated. The coffee tree bears both ripe (red) and unripe (green) "cherries" simultaneously, so coffee cherries must be picked by hand.

Lime Liquado with Mint

You find the most wonderful fruit and ice shakes in Mexico that are called liquados. This is a new twist on a traditional favorite.

2	cups	water	500	mL
½	cup	frozen limeade	125	mL
¼	cup	fresh mint leaves	60	mL
12		ice cubes	12	
		lime twists, for garnish		

Combine all ingredients in a blender and process until smooth. Serve in tall highball glasses and garnish each glass with a lime twist.

Serves 2.

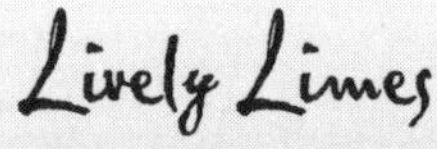

Lively Limes

The tart and tangy flavor of the versatile lime adds a sprightly touch to margaritas, other fruit drinks and desserts. It adds zest to seviche, salad dressings, barbecued fish and poultry. An excellent source of vitamin C, limes grow in the tropics and subtropics, Mexico, the Caribbean, Florida and California.

Watermelon Margaritas, page 26

Strawberry-Banana Batidos

Like "liquados" in Mexico, Cuba is noted for these colorful and refreshing fruit smoothies that are called "batidos" which literally translates as "whipped" in English.

1	cup	ripe strawberries (frozen may be substituted)	250	mL
2		ripe bananas	2	
2	tbsp.	sugar	30	mL
1½	cups	skim milk	375	mL
		ice		
2		strawberries, for garnish	2	

Combine all ingredients in a blender and process until smooth. Pour over ice in tall highball glasses and garnish each glass with a strawberry.

Serves 2.

Variations: Blueberries may be substituted for strawberries in this recipe.

Strawberries

A member of the rose family, strawberries grew wild in North and South America and Europe until the late 1800s when they began to be cultivated. Store fresh strawberries in the refrigerator, in a single layer on paper towels if possible, and in a covered container. Don't rinse them until you are ready to use them and don't remove the hulls until serving time. High in vitamin C, strawberries also contain iron and potassium. Strawberries have an affinity for cream, orange and red wine, and for we fiery food lovers, strawberries are divine with balsamic vinegar and freshly ground pepper.

Mexican Hot Chocolate

1/2	cup	unsweetened cocoa powder	125	mL
1/4	cup	brown sugar, preferably dark	60	mL
4	cups	skim milk	1	L
4		cinnamon sticks	4	
1/4	tsp.	ground cloves	1	mL
1	tsp.	vanilla extract	5	mL
1/2	cup	Kahlúa liqueur (optional)	125	mL
		whipped cream, for garnish (optional)		
		ground cinnamon, for garnish		

In a medium saucepan, combine cocoa powder, sugar and just enough milk to make a thick paste. Add remaining milk, cinnamon sticks and cloves. Bring to a boil over medium heat, stirring constantly. Simmer for 5 minutes. Remove from heat.

Remove cinnamon sticks from saucepan and place 1 stick in each of 4 serving mugs. To hot chocolate mixture in saucepan, stir in vanilla and Kahlúa, if desired. Pour into mugs and garnish with whipped cream and a sprinkle of cinnamon.

Serves 4.

Pictured on page 143

Chocolate

Mexico is the birthplace of chocolate (thank you for such a wonderful gift to the world!). It was revered by the Aztecs and was served exclusively to priests and kings with such additions as herbs, chiles and honey. Although the hot chocolate of Mexico is famous throughout the world, they are also well known for their use of chocolate in a sauce called mole, where it is used as one of many spices.

BREADS

Lemon Ginger Scones

Ginger is deliciously hot and is unusual because it has an affinity with both savory and sweet foods. Asian cultures have long believed in ginger's ability to alleviate many specific illnesses and promote overall vitality and well-being. Try these scones for brunch with the Margarita Fruit Salad featured on page 14.

2	cups	all-purpose flour	500	mL
1/4	cup	sugar	60	mL
1	tsp.	baking soda	5	mL
1	tsp.	cream of tartar	5	mL
1/4	cup	finely chopped crystallized ginger	60	mL
2	tsp.	grated lemon zest	10	mL
1	cup	buttermilk	250	mL
1	tbsp.	canola oil	15	mL
1		egg	1	
1	tbsp.	water	15	mL
1	tbsp.	sugar	15	mL

Preheat oven to 350°F (180°C).

In a medium bowl, mix together flour, 1/4 cup (60 mL) of sugar, baking soda and cream of tartar. Stir in ginger and lemon zest.

In a small bowl, combine buttermilk and oil and add to the dry ingredients, stirring just until blended. Turn the slightly sticky dough out onto a lightly floured work surface and pat to 1/2" (1.3 cm) thickness. Using a floured 4" (10 cm) round cutter, cut out the dough. Cut each circle in half to make half-moons. Reroll and cut the scraps, handling the dough as little as possible. Place scones onto a baking sheet that has been lightly oiled or coated with nonstick cooking spray.

In a small bowl, lightly beat the egg with the water. Brush the tops of the scones with the egg glaze. Sprinkle scones with 1 tbsp. (15 mL) of sugar.

Bake for 15 to 20 minutes, or until the tops are golden and firm to touch. Serve warm.

Makes about 16 scones.

Tempting Two-Pepper Biscuits

2	cups	self-rising flour* (variety baking mix like Bisquick or Tea-Bisk)	500	mL
2		serrano or jalapeño peppers, finely chopped	2	
1/2	tsp.	coarsely ground black pepper	2	mL
2	tbsp.	grated Parmesan cheese	30	mL
1/2	tsp.	dried oregano	2	mL
2	tbsp.	vegetable shortening (like Tenderflake)	30	mL
1	cup	buttermilk	250	mL

Preheat oven to 425°F (220°C).

Combine the flour, serrano pepper, black pepper, Parmesan cheese and oregano in a large bowl until well mixed. Using a fork or pastry cutter, cut the shortening into the flour. Make a well in the center of the flour mixture and add the buttermilk, a little at a time, stirring, until all the flour is incorporated and a fairly stiff dough is formed.

Place the dough on a floured surface; knead into a ball and sprinkle with additional flour as required. Roll out the dough to 3/4" (2 cm) thickness. Cut out 3" (8 cm) biscuits and place on an ungreased baking sheet.

Bake for 15 to 18 minutes, or until lightly browned.

Makes 12 large biscuits.

* To make self-rising flour, add 1 1/2 tsp. (7 mL) of baking powder and 1/3 tsp. (1.5 mL) of salt to 1 cup (250 mL) of flour.

Hot Peppers!

The heat of chiles and peppers is caused by a substance called capsaicin. Capsaicin is a flavorless, odorless chemical concentrated in the veins of chiles and peppers. The seeds grow next to the veins and absorb the chemical (removing seeds and veins can reduce heat by up to fifty percent). Otherwise, capsaicin is virtually indestructible and can withstand freezing, cooking and time.

Experts believe that capsaicin acts on nerve fibers that carry pain signals throughout the nervous system. If you've ever accidentally touched your eye or lip after handling hot peppers, you'll know what I mean! See the capsaicin note on medicinal uses on page 31 and health benefits on page 131.

Banana Bran Muffins with a Bite

These are not only healthy, but delicious with the combination of "sweet" and "heat".

1¼	cups	all-purpose flour	300	mL
½	cup	natural bran	125	mL
⅓	cup	wheat germ	75	mL
1	tsp.	baking powder	5	mL
1	tsp.	baking soda	5	mL
½	cup	butter or margarine	125	mL
½	cup	lightly packed brown sugar	125	mL
1		egg	1	
⅔	cup	mashed banana (approximately 3 bananas)	150	mL
½	cup	buttermilk	125	mL
2	tbsp.	molasses	30	mL
2		jalapeño peppers, finely chopped	2	
¾	cup	raisins	175	mL
⅓	cup	chopped nuts or millet (optional)	75	mL
2	tbsp.	flax seed (optional)	30	mL

Preheat oven to 375°F (190°C).

In a large bowl, combine flour, bran, wheat germ, baking powder and soda.

In a medium bowl, cream butter, brown sugar and egg together until light and fluffy. Add mashed banana, buttermilk and molasses; mix well.

Add liquid ingredients all at once to dry ingredients. Stir just until all ingredients are moistened. Stir in jalapeño pepper, raisins, nuts or millet and flax seed.

Coat muffin cups with nonstick cooking spray; fill ¾ full. Bake for 20 to 25 minutes, or until tops of muffins spring back when lightly touched.

Makes 12 large muffins.

Orange Habañero Muffins

These muffins have quite a kick! Remember that the habañero is the world's hottest chile (wear rubber gloves when handling), so cut back to half a chile if you'll be serving to someone with a delicate palate! For the really faint at heart, the habañero can be cut out completely for a simple and delicious sweet muffin!

1		whole orange, washed, cut in quarters and seeded	1	
1		whole habañero chile, washed and cut in half	1	
1/2	cup	butter or margarine	125	mL
1		egg	1	
1 1/2	cups	all-purpose flour	375	mL
3/4	cup	sugar	175	mL
1	tsp.	baking powder	5	mL
1	tsp.	baking soda	5	mL
1/2	cup	orange juice	125	mL
1/2	cup	chopped, pitted dates	125	mL
1/2	cup	chopped pecans	125	mL

Preheat oven to 400°F (200°C).

Place orange and habañero into the bowl of a food processor and process until smooth. Add the butter and egg and process until smooth. Add flour, sugar, baking powder, baking soda and orange juice and process until just mixed. Scrape down sides of bowl and add dates and pecans. Process until just combined.

Spoon batter into muffin cups that have been coated with nonstick cooking spray. Bake for 15 minutes, or until tops of muffins spring back when lightly touched.

Makes 12 large muffins.

Metabolism Boosters

Research has proven that adding chile peppers to your foods can help your body burn calories faster (up to 45 calories more per meal than if you eat bland dishes).

Cheesy Chile Corn Muffins

Add Salsa Cream Cheese, page 48, for a brunch or breakfast treat.

1	cup	all-purpose flour	250	mL
1	cup	cornmeal	250	mL
1	tbsp.	granulated sugar	15	mL
1	tbsp.	baking powder	15	mL
½	tsp.	baking soda	2	mL
1¼	cups	shredded old Cheddar cheese	310	mL
1½	cups	frozen whole-kernel corn	375	mL
½		large red bell pepper, finely chopped	½	
1		jalapeño pepper, minced	1	
2		eggs, lightly beaten	2	
1	cup	buttermilk	250	mL
¼	cup	vegetable oil	60	mL
¼	cup	shredded old Cheddar cheese	60	mL

Preheat oven to 400°F (200°C).

In a large bowl, combine flour, cornmeal, sugar, baking powder and baking soda; mix thoroughly. Stir in first Cheddar cheese, corn, red and jalapeño peppers and make a well in the center of the ingredients.

In a small bowl, combine eggs, buttermilk and oil. Add to corn mixture; stir until just combined.

Spoon batter into 12 greased muffin tins or cornbread molds. Sprinkle with remaining Cheddar cheese. Bake for 16 to 18 minutes, or until a tester inserted in the center comes out clean.

Makes 12 muffins.

Pictured on page 17.

Chile Highs

When people eat hotter chiles, they experience pain in their mouths and throats. The nervous system reacts to the pain by releasing morphine-like endorphins. Endorphins create a sense of euphoria similar to the "runner's high" that some people get from exercise. People who regularly eat chiles will find that they develop a tolerance to the heat and will have to eat increasingly hotter foods to get the high.

Pan-Roasted Chipotle Corn Bread

1/2	tsp.	vegetable oil	2	mL
1		medium onion, chopped	1	
2		garlic cloves, minced	2	
1	cup	frozen whole-kernel corn, thawed	250	mL
1	tsp.	ground chipotle chile powder	5	mL
1	tsp.	vegetable oil	5	mL
1 1/4	cups	cornmeal	310	mL
3/4	cup	all-purpose flour	175	mL
2 1/2	tsp.	baking powder	12	mL
1/2	tsp.	baking soda	2	mL
1 1/2	cups	buttermilk	375	mL
1 1/2	tbsp.	butter or margarine, melted	22	mL
1		egg, lightly beaten	1	
1		egg white, lightly beaten	1	

Preheat oven to 425°F (220°C).

Heat 1/2 tsp. (2 mL) vegetable oil in a 9" (23 cm) cast-iron skillet over medium-high heat. Add onion and garlic; sauté for 5 minutes, or until onion is translucent. Add corn and chipotle chile powder; sauté for 4 minutes, or until lightly browned. Place onion and corn mixture in a bowl and set aside.

Coat bottom and sides of skillet with remaining 1 tsp. (5 mL) vegetable oil. Place in oven for 5 minutes, or until hot.

Combine cornmeal, flour, baking powder and baking soda in a large bowl. Combine onion and corn mixture, buttermilk, butter, egg and egg white; stir well. Add to cornmeal mixture and stir just until all ingredients are moistened.

Pour batter into preheated skillet and bake for 25 minutes, or until a tester inserted into the center comes out clean.

Makes 10 servings.

Jalapeño Cheese Loaf

This loaf is wonderful served with soup, chili or salad.

1	cup	all-purpose flour	250	mL
1/2	cup	cornmeal	125	mL
1/2	tsp.	baking soda	2	mL
1/4	tsp.	black pepper	1	mL
3/4	cup	low-fat plain yogurt	175	mL
1/4	cup	vegetable oil	60	mL
1		egg, lightly beaten	1	
1	cup	grated zucchini	250	mL
1	cup	shredded Monterey Jack cheese	250	mL
2		jalapeño peppers, finely chopped	2	

Preheat oven to 350°F (180°C).

In a small bowl, combine flour, cornmeal, baking soda and black pepper; set aside.

In a medium bowl, stir together yogurt, oil and egg until well combined. Stir in zucchini, cheese and jalapeño pepper.

Add dry ingredients all at once; stir just until dry ingredients are moistened (do not overmix). Spoon batter into an 4 x 8" (10 x 20 cm) loaf pan that has been coated with nonstick cooking spray.

Bake for about 60 minutes, or until golden brown and a tester inserted in the center comes out clean. Let cool in pan for 10 minutes; remove from pan and place on cutting board. Serve warm.

Makes 1 loaf (approximately 12 slices).

Pumpkin Bread with Cranberries

Try this with the Cranberry-Orange Cream Cheese featured on page 48.

1/2	cup	all-purpose flour	125	mL
1/2	cup	whole-wheat flour	125	mL
1/2	cup	cornmeal	125	mL
1	cup	packed brown sugar	250	mL
2	tsp.	baking powder	10	mL
1	tsp.	baking soda	5	mL
1	tsp.	ground cinnamon	5	mL
1/2	tsp.	ground ginger	2	mL
1	cup	plain pumpkin purée	250	mL
1/2	cup	low-fat plain yogurt	125	mL
1/4	cup	vegetable oil	60	mL
1		large egg	1	
1		large egg white	1	
1	cup	dried cranberries	250	mL

Preheat oven to 350°F (180°C). Coat a 5 x 9" (13 x 23 cm) loaf pan with nonstick cooking spray.

In a large bowl, combine white and whole-wheat flours, cornmeal, brown sugar, baking powder, baking soda, cinnamon and ginger; mix thoroughly.

In another bowl, whisk together pumpkin, yogurt, oil, egg and egg white until well combined.

Stir the pumpkin mixture and cranberries into the dry ingredients until just completely blended. Pour the batter into the loaf pan and smooth the top with a spatula.

Bake for 55 to 60 minutes, or until a tester inserted in the center comes out clean. Let the loaf rest in the pan for 5 minutes then turn it onto a wire rack to cool completely.

Makes 1 loaf (approximately 12 slices).

Pictured on page 143.

Cranberry-Orange Cream Cheese

8	oz.	light cream cheese	250	g
1/2	cup	dried cranberries	125	mL
2	tbsp.	orange-flavored liqueur (Triple Sec, Cointreau or Grand Marnier)	30	mL
2	tsp.	grated fresh orange zest	10	mL

Blend all ingredients in a small bowl.

Makes about 1 1/3 cups (325 mL).

Pictured on page 143.

Salsa Cream Cheese

Try this cream cheese spread on Cheesy Chile Corn Muffins, page 44, or on a toasted bagel for breakfast.

1/2	cup	medium chunky salsa	125	mL
8	oz.	light cream cheese, softened	250	g
1	tsp.	ground cumin	5	mL

Place salsa in a strainer and press out most of the liquid.

Thoroughly blend salsa, cream cheese and ground cumin in a small bowl.

Makes about 1 1/3 cups (325 mL).

APPETIZERS

Grilled Quesadillas

I've found that the best quesadillas are those that are cooked on the barbecue grill. Try a couple of these combinations for your next summer brunch or as appetizers for a casual dinner with friends.

Pesto Quesadillas:

4		10" (25 cm) flour tortillas	4	
1/4	cup	cilantro pesto (see page 103 for recipe)	60	mL
1/2	cup	diced yellow bell pepper	125	mL
1/2	cup	diced red bell pepper	125	mL
1/2	cup	shredded Monterey Jack cheese	125	mL

Sun-Dried Tomato with Brie Quesadillas:

4		10" (25 cm) flour tortillas	4	
4	oz.	Brie cheese	120	g
1/4	cup	chopped reconstituted sun-dried tomatoes	60	mL
1/4	cup	chopped pecans, toasted	60	mL

Roasted Red Pepper Quesadillas:

4		10" (25 cm) flour tortillas	4	
4	oz.	soft goat cheese or feta cheese	120	g
1/4	cup	chopped roasted red bell peppers (see page 58 for instructions)	60	mL
1		green onion, finely sliced	1	
2	tbsp.	sliced black olives	30	mL

Mexican Quesadillas:

4		10" (25 cm) flour tortillas	4	
1/2	cup	refried beans or mashed kidney beans	125	mL
1/2	cup	shredded Monterey Jack cheese	125	mL
2		jalapeño peppers, finely chopped	2	
2	tbsp.	chopped fresh cilantro	30	mL

Preheat barbecue to medium heat.

For each of the combinations shown above, spread fillings evenly over half of each of the tortillas. Fold over, toast on the grill on both sides until lightly browned and cheese is melted. Remove from grill, cut each quesadilla into quarters and enjoy!

Each combination serves 8 (2 wedges per person).

Black Bean Roll-Ups

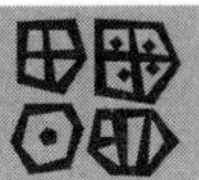

2	tsp.	ground cumin	10	mL
1	tsp.	dried oregano	5	mL
1	tbsp.	vegetable oil	15	mL
1		large onion, finely chopped	1	
3		garlic cloves, minced	3	
2		jalapeño peppers, finely chopped	2	
2x19	oz.	cans black beans, drained and rinsed	2x540	mL
3	tbsp.	dry white wine	45	mL
2	tbsp.	red wine vinegar	30	mL
1	tbsp.	sun-dried tomato paste	15	mL
		black pepper, to taste		
6		10" (25 cm) flour tortillas	6	
		salsa		
		sour cream		

In a large nonstick skillet, add cumin and oregano and toast over medium heat, stirring constantly, until fragrant but not browned. Remove from skillet and set aside.

Heat oil over medium heat. Add onions, garlic and jalapeños; cook until onions are golden brown, stirring frequently. Stir in beans, wine, vinegar, tomato paste and toasted cumin and oregano. Cook for about 5 to 10 minutes, stirring occasionally, until the beans are soft and begin to break down. Season with black pepper to taste.

Heat each tortilla for 30 seconds per side in a nonstick skillet over medium heat.

Lay a warmed tortilla on a flat work surface. Spread 1/2 cup (125 mL) of the bean mixture on the tortilla to within 1/2" (1.3 cm) of the outside edge. Roll up into a tight roll. Repeat with remaining tortillas and beans.

Slice the rolls diagonally into 1" (2.5 cm) lengths. Keep roll-ups warm in 200°F (93°C) oven until you are ready to serve them. Arrange the slices on a serving platter, and serve with salsa and sour cream.

Makes approximately 48 appetizers.

Tortilla Torte

This recipe, if you're serving several appetizers, is a great shortcut to create another dish if you're already making the White Bean Dip or Roasted Red Pepper Hummus.

3		10" (25 cm) flour tortillas	3	
1/2	cup	White Bean Dip (see page 60 for recipe) or Roasted Red Pepper Hummus (see page 61 for recipe)	125	mL
1/2	cup	shredded light Cheddar cheese	125	mL
		Tomatillo Chipotle Salsa (see page 153) or Charred Pico de Gallo (see page 151)		

Preheat oven to 400°F (200°C).

Spread 1/4 cup (60 mL) of White Bean Dip or Roasted Red Pepper Hummus and sprinkle 1/4 cup (60 mL) of Cheddar cheese on each of 2 tortillas. Stack 1 tortilla on top of the other; finishing by stacking the third tortilla on top.

Place on a baking sheet and cook for 10 minutes, or until cheese melts. Cut into 8 wedges and serve with either Tomatillo Chipotle Salsa or Charred Pico de Gallo.

Serves 8.

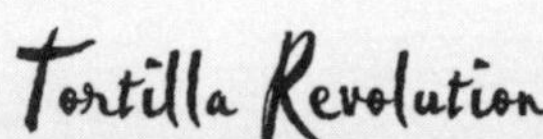

Tortilla Revolution

According to the Tortilla Industry Association, tortillas are the fastest growing portion of the baking industry in the United States. In 1995, Americans spent more than 2 billion dollars and ate about 60 million tortillas. That equates to approximately 225 tortillas per person which is more than bagels, pitas and English muffins combined!

Appetizers

Mexican Bruschetta, page 58

Tartas Con Chorizo

A sure hit to serve at parties!

6		10" (25 cm) flour tortillas, cut in quarters	6	
2	tbsp.	olive oil	30	mL
6	oz.	chorizo sausage, casings removed and cut into ½" (1.3 cm) slices (require 24 pieces)	170	g
4		eggs, lightly beaten	4	
13½	oz.	can evaporated skim milk	385	mL
1	tbsp.	chopped fresh cilantro	15	mL
1	tsp.	red chile powder	5	mL
½	tsp.	ground cumin	2	mL
¼	tsp.	hot pepper sauce	1	mL
1½	cups	shredded Monterey Jack cheese	375	mL
1		small red onion, very thinly sliced, cut in half and separated into rings	1	
4	oz.	can chopped green chiles, drained	114	mL

Preheat oven to 375°F (190°C).

Cut tortillas. Using a pastry brush, lightly brush olive oil over both sides of the tortilla quarters. Place tortilla quarters in muffin tins that have been coated with nonstick cooking spray. Bake for 10 minutes. Remove from oven and set aside.

In a large nonstick skillet, cook chorizo over medium heat until well browned. Remove chorizo from skillet and place on a plate between sheets of paper towel. Blot all grease off chorizo, then place 1 slice of chorizo in each tortilla cup.

In a medium bowl, combine eggs, milk, cilantro, chile powder, cumin and hot pepper sauce until well blended. Pour egg mixture over chorizo in the tortilla cups; evenly distribute cheese, onion rings and green chiles over egg mixture.

Bake for 15 to 20 minutes, or until egg mixture is firm to the touch.

Makes 24 tarts.

Artichoke and Feta Cheese Roll with Roasted Red Pepper Sauce

Roasted Red Pepper Sauce:

2		roasted red bell peppers (see page 58 for instructions), chopped	2	
1	tbsp.	olive oil	15	mL
2		celery stalks, chopped	2	
1		small onion, chopped	1	
1½	tsp.	dried thyme	7	mL
¼	cup	vegetable stock	60	mL
2	tbsp.	dry sherry	30	mL
1	tbsp.	balsamic vinegar	15	mL
		black pepper, to taste		

Artichoke and Feta Cheese Roll:

1	tbsp.	olive oil	15	mL
1		medium onion, chopped	1	
3		garlic cloves, minced	3	
2x14	oz.	cans artichoke hearts, chopped	2x398	g
1	tbsp.	dried basil	15	mL
¼	cup	dry white wine	60	mL
1	cup	crumbled feta cheese	250	mL
		black pepper, to taste		
8		sheets phyllo pastry, thawed	8	
6	tbsp.	butter, melted	90	mL

Roast red peppers. In a large nonstick skillet, heat 1 tbsp. (15 mL) olive oil over medium-high heat. Add celery, onion and thyme and sauté until vegetables are tender, about 8 minutes. Add vegetable stock, sherry and roasted peppers. Simmer for about 10 minutes, or until almost all liquid evaporates. Purée mixture in food processor or blender until smooth. Transfer to a medium saucepan, and stir in balsamic vinegar. Season sauce to taste with black pepper and set aside.

In a large nonstick skillet, heat 1 tbsp. (15 mL) olive oil over medium-high heat. Add onion and garlic and sauté until onion is tender, about 4 minutes. Add artichoke hearts, basil and wine. Simmer until almost all liquid evaporates, then remove from heat and cool completely. Stir in feta cheese and season with black pepper to taste.

Place 1 phyllo sheet on work surface with the long edge parallel to the edge of the work surface. Be sure to keep remaining sheets of phyllo pastry covered (with a damp tea towel) as they will dry out very quickly.

Artichoke and Feta Cheese Roll with Roasted Red Pepper Sauce continued

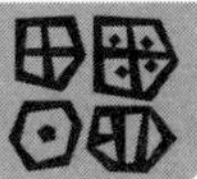

Lightly brush the first sheet of phyllo pastry with melted butter. Top with another phyllo sheet and brush with butter. Repeat layering with remaining phyllo sheets and butter. Spoon filling in a 2" (5 cm) wide strip near bottom edge of phyllo, leaving a 2" (5 cm) border at the bottom and sides. Fold bottom edge over filling. Fold short sides in. Roll up like a jelly roll. Place seam side down on a large baking sheet, and brush with butter.

Bake roll in a preheated 400°F (200°C) oven until golden, about 20 minutes. Transfer pan to rack and cool slightly.

Rewarm sauce over low heat. Cut roll into 2" (5 cm) wide slices, and serve warm with Roasted Red Pepper Sauce.

Serves 6 to 8.

Southwestern Cheese Toast

Although this recipe is not low in fat, serve it as an appetizer treat or combine it with a low-fat soup or salad for a casual and satisfying dinner combination.

1	cup	shredded light Cheddar cheese	250	mL
1/2	cup	cubed light cream cheese	125	mL
1/4	cup	chopped fresh parsley	60	mL
1		jalapeño pepper, finely chopped	1	
1/4	tsp.	cayenne pepper	1	mL
2-3	tbsp.	milk	30-45	mL
1		baguette loaf, sliced	1	

Preheat oven to 375°F (190°C).

In a food processor, combine cheeses and process until smooth. Add parsley, jalapeño, cayenne pepper and milk; process to combine.

Spread 1 to 2 tsp. (5 to 10 mL) of cheese mixture on each baguette slice and place on an ungreased baking sheet.

Bake 10 to 12 minutes, or until cheese topping is puffed and golden brown.

Serves 8.

Mexican Bruschetta

4		Roma tomatoes, chopped	4	
2		red bell peppers, roasted, peeled, seeded and chopped (see instructions below)	2	
1	tsp.	pickled jalapeño peppers, finely chopped	5	mL
1/4	cup	sliced black olives	60	mL
2		garlic cloves, minced	2	
1	tbsp.	balsamic vinegar	15	mL
1	tbsp.	olive oil	15	mL
1/4	cup	chopped fresh basil	60	mL
1/8	tsp.	black pepper	0.5	mL
		foccacia bread or toasted baguette bread		
1/2	cup	shredded Monterey Jack cheese	125	mL

Preheat oven to 400°F (200°C).

In a medium bowl, stir together all ingredients, except bread and cheese. Spread on top of foccacia bread or toasted baguette bread, and sprinkle with cheese.

Place on baking sheet and bake for 15 to 20 minutes. Slice and serve.

Serves 8.

Pictured on page 53.

Roasting Red Peppers

To roast red peppers, place whole peppers on a barbecue and grill, turning frequently, until the entire pepper surface is blackened. Remove from grill, place in a covered bowl or plastic bag and let cool. Peel off the skin and remove the stems, cores and seeds.

You can also roast red peppers in the oven. Cut the peppers in half lengthwise and remove core and seeds. Place peppers on a baking sheet covered with aluminum foil. Flatten peppers with palm of hand, skin side up, and grill them under a broiler in the oven until blistered and blackened. Remove from oven; place in a covered bowl or plastic bag and let cool. Peel and chop peppers.

Roasted peppers freeze very well, so we usually pick up a case or 2 from the Farmer's Market in the fall and put away a supply to last the year, packaged in small quantities in plastic bags.

Jícama with Lime and Red Chile

This is an informal appetizer that is meant to be shared by a group of special people.

1		medium jícama, peeled and cut in julienne slices 1/4" (1 cm) thick	1	
1		English cucumber, washed and cut into 1/4" (1 cm) diagonal slices	1	
4		seedless navel oranges, peeled, split into quarters, then cut crosswise into 1/4" (1 cm) slices	4	
6		radishes, cut in half lengthwise and then crosswise into 1/4" (1 cm) slices	6	
2		fresh limes, juice of	2	
2	tsp.	red chile powder	10	mL
		cilantro sprigs, for garnish		

In a large bowl, mix together jícama, cucumber, oranges, radishes and lime juice. Allow to marinate for 30 minutes.

Transfer vegetables and juice to a serving platter. Sprinkle with the chile powder and garnish with cilantro sprigs.

Serves 8.

Jícama

Jícama (pronounced hée-ca-ma) is a brown-skinned, rough looking tuberous vegetable (resembles a turnip in shape) which is normally eaten raw. It has a crisp, juicy texture and the flavor is a delightful combination of freshly picked peas and water chestnuts. Jícama makes a wonderful snack either on its own or with a squeeze of fresh lime and a sprinkle of red chile powder (great for packed lunches).

Jícama is available in most large supermarkets or specialty produce stores. Select smaller jícama (less than 1 lb. [500 g]) that are firm and unshriveled as they are younger and sweeter in flavor. You can store jícama for up to 1 week in the refrigerator crisper.

Peel off the skin and approximately 1/8" (3 mm) just below the skin. Slice or dice the jícama to serve or use in recipes.

White Bean Dip

19	oz.	can white kidney beans, drained and rinsed	540	mL
8	oz.	package light cream cheese	250	g
¼	cup	fat-free sour cream	60	mL
2		garlic cloves, minced	2	
1	tsp.	grated lime rind	5	mL
¼	cup	lime juice	60	mL
1	tbsp.	red chile powder	15	mL
1	tsp.	dried oregano	5	mL
1	tsp.	hot pepper flakes	5	mL

Garnish:

chopped tomato, chopped green onion, shredded light Cheddar cheese, fat-free sour cream

In a food processor, combine all ingredients, except garnishes, and process until smooth. Transfer to a serving bowl; cover and refrigerate for at least 2 hours.

To serve, place a ring of chopped tomato on top of bean dip, around outside edge of serving bowl. Inside the tomato ring, place a ring of chopped green onion, followed by a ring of Cheddar cheese and finished with a dollop of sour cream in the center of the bowl.

Serve with Baked Tortilla Chips, page 160, or bagel chips.

Makes 2½ cups (625 mL).

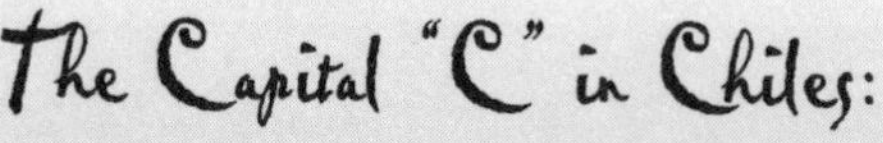

The Capital "C" in Chiles:

Fresh chiles offer the highest source of vitamin C available from any vegetable. Surprisingly, they provide twice the amount that is available from citrus fruits.

Roasted Red Pepper Hummus

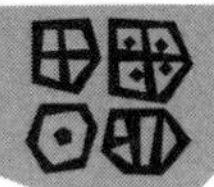

This recipe was inspired by the good folks at The Cookbook Company Cooks in Calgary, who prepared a similar hummus for a corporate function held at our office. This makes a great dip for fresh vegetables, mini whole-wheat pitas, Baked Tortilla Chips (see page 160 for recipe), papadams, or as a spread in pita sandwiches or wraps.

2		garlic cloves, peeled	2	
3		red bell peppers, roasted, peeled, seeded and chopped (see page 58 for instructions)	3	
19	oz.	can garbanzo beans, drained and rinsed	540	mL
3	tbsp.	fresh lemon juice	45	mL
2	tbsp.	tahini or smooth peanut butter	30	mL
1	tsp.	ground cumin	5	mL
½	tsp.	cayenne pepper or hot pepper sauce	2	mL
3	tbsp.	chopped cilantro or parsley	45	mL

Place garlic cloves in the bowl of a food processor and process until finely minced. Place peeled peppers, garbanzo beans, lemon juice, tahini, cumin and cayenne pepper in food processor and process until smooth. Scrape down the sides of the bowl as necessary. Add cilantro and pulse quickly to mix.

Place in a serving bowl and allow to sit for 30 minutes before serving to allow flavors to blend. Garnish with a sprig of cilantro to serve.

Makes about 2 cups (500 mL).

Chili Con Queso

Try serving this dish at your next large gathering with bread, fresh vegetables or tortilla chips.

16	oz.	process cheese (like Velveeta), cubed	500	g
8	oz.	sharp Cheddar cheese, shredded	250	g
8		garlic cloves, minced	8	
1		onion, finely chopped	1	
6		serrano or jalapeño peppers, finely chopped	6	
14	oz.	can diced tomatoes	398	mL

Preheat oven to 225°F (107°C).

Place cheeses, garlic, onion, peppers and tomatoes in a large ovenproof dish that has been coated with nonstick cooking spray. Mix together until well blended. Place in oven and bake for 2 hours, stirring 3 or 4 times. Serve hot in a chafing dish or in a ceramic fondue pot.

Serves lots!

Vitamin Source

Chiles are a good source of vitamins A and C. As chiles turn from green to red, they lose much of their vitamin C but gain vitamin A through increased amounts of carotene.

Garlic and Cheese Stuffed Mushrooms

4	oz.	soft goat cheese	120	g
4		garlic cloves, minced	4	
2	tsp.	fresh lime juice	10	mL
1	tbsp.	chopped fresh cilantro or parsley	15	mL
		black pepper, to taste		
1	lb	large fresh mushrooms	500	g

Preheat oven to 350°F (180°C).

In a small bowl, mix together goat cheese, garlic, lime juice, cilantro and black pepper to taste.

Remove stems from mushrooms. Wipe mushrooms with a damp cloth to clean. Fill mushroom centers with cheese mixture. Place mushrooms on a baking sheet that has been coated with nonstick cooking spray.

Bake for 20 minutes, or until mushrooms are soft.

Serves 6.

Cilantro

Cilantro, otherwise known as coriander or Chinese parsley, is an herb that is widely used in Mexican, Thai and many other cuisines of the world, both as a primary ingredient and as a beautiful garnish. It has a very distinctive flavor and aroma that people seem to either love or hate. If you truly dislike the flavor, fresh parsley may be substituted in most recipes.

Cilantro has become as affordable as parsley and is readily available in most supermarkets. To store both cilantro and parsley, re-cut the stems and place in a glass with ½" (1.3 cm) water in the bottom, cover with plastic and place in the refrigerator (will keep for up to a week).

Baked Brie with Roasted Garlic

This recipe is a blend of flavors inspired by dishes enjoyed at the St. Francis Hotel in Santa Fe and the Tullamore restaurant in Calgary.

7	oz.	pkg. frozen puff pastry, thawed	200	g
4	oz.	Brie cheese	120	g
1	head	roasted garlic (see page 81 for instructions)	1	head
½	cup	jalapeño pepper jelly	125	mL

Preheat oven to 400°F (200°C).

On a lightly floured surface, roll pastry into a 9" (23 cm) square. Place whole round of Brie in the center and squeeze roasted garlic onto top of cheese. Pull up sides of pastry and lightly press edges to seal (there should be sufficient pastry to mold an interesting design on top). Place on baking sheet and bake for 20 minutes, or until pastry is evenly browned.

Place whole pastry on serving dish and pour jalapeño pepper jelly over top. Serve with melba toast, tortilla chips or gourmet crackers. You'll want to have side plates, forks and napkins available as the jalapeño jelly makes this a bit messy. Have guests cut into the Brie themselves for their desired portion.

Serves 4 to 6.

Baked Artichoke-Parmesan Dip

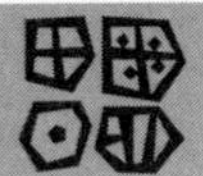

This recipe can be made well ahead and is always popular. Great to take if you've been asked to bring an appetizer to a friend's home or to make the night before a dinner party.

2		garlic cloves, peeled	2	
14	oz.	can artichoke hearts, drained	398	mL
1	cup	grated Parmesan cheese	250	mL
1/4	cup	low-fat mayonnaise	60	mL
1	tsp.	grated lemon zest	5	mL
1/4	tsp.	cayenne pepper	1	mL
		black pepper, to taste		
1	tbsp.	chopped fresh parsley, for garnish	15	mL

Preheat oven to 400°F (200°C).

In a food processor, add garlic and process until finely minced. Add artichoke hearts, Parmesan cheese, mayonnaise, lemon zest and cayenne pepper; process until smooth. Scrape down the sides of the processor bowl with a spatula and add black pepper to taste.

Transfer mixture to a small ovenproof dish and bake for 20 minutes. Garnish with parsley and serve warm with Baked Tortilla Chips (see page 160) or toasted slices of baguette.

Makes about 1 1/2 cups (375 mL).

Santa Fe Snack Mix

This mix is incredibly addictive but so good! Makes a great hostess gift or packaged for those special people at Christmas.

¾	cup	butter	175	mL
¼	cup	hot pepper sauce (like Louisiana Hot Sauce)	60	mL
¼	cup	Worcestershire sauce	60	mL
2	tbsp.	red chile powder	30	mL
1	tsp.	chipotle chile powder	5	mL
4	tbsp.	garlic powder	60	mL
1	tbsp.	onion powder	15	mL
8	cups	box Crispix cereal	2	L
8	cups	box Cheerios cereal	2	L
8	cups	box Shreddies cereal	2	L
2	cups	corn chips	500	mL
2	cups	corn nuts	500	mL
2	cups	box Ritz Bits mini cheese crackers or Goldfish crackers	500	mL
2	cups	mini pretzels or pretzel sticks	500	mL
2	cups	unsalted peanuts	500	mL

Preheat oven to 250°F (120°C).

In a large roasting pan, melt butter with hot pepper sauce, Worcestershire sauce, chile powders, garlic powder and onion powder.

In a large bowl, stir together remaining ingredients. Pour melted butter mixture over cereal mixture and toss to coat thoroughly. Transfer mixture to roasting pan and place in oven. Bake for 1½ hours, stirring every 10 to 15 minutes.

Transfer mixture to storage container(s), cool completely, then cover tightly. Store at room temperature for up to 2 weeks.

Serves many!

SALADS

Bueno Broccoli Salad

2	tbsp.	red wine vinegar	30	mL
2	tbsp.	olive oil	30	mL
½	cup	orange juice	125	mL
2	tsp.	Dijon mustard	10	mL
½	tsp.	ground cumin	2	mL
	dash	black pepper	dash	
3	cups	broccoli florets	750	mL
1		small jícama, cut in julienne slices	1	
12	oz.	can whole-kernel corn, drained and rinsed	341	mL
1		medium red bell pepper, chopped	1	
1		small red onion, chopped	1	

In a small bowl, whisk together vinegar, oil, orange juice, mustard, cumin and black pepper. Set aside.

In a large bowl, combine broccoli, jícama, corn, red pepper and onion. Stir dressing; pour over salad and toss to coat. Cover and refrigerate at least 3 hours. Toss again before serving.

Serves 8.

Pictured on page 71.

Smaller is Hotter

The general rule is that the smaller a chile pepper is, the hotter it is.

Jícama Mango Coleslaw

This is a simple yet flavorful salad. A tasty twist on traditional coleslaw.

3	cups	shredded cabbage	750	mL
1		medium jícama, peeled and shredded	1	
1		mango, chopped	1	
2		green onions, chopped	2	
1		lime, juice of	1	

Combine cabbage, jícama, mango and green onions. Sprinkle with lime juice and stir to combine.

Serves 6.

Piquant Vinaigrette

2	tbsp.	olive oil	30	mL
2	tbsp.	apple cider vinegar	30	mL
1	tsp.	hot pepper flakes	5	mL
1	tsp.	red chile powder	5	mL
1/2	tsp.	ground cumin	2	mL

Stir all ingredients together and serve over your favorite salad greens.

Makes 1/4 cup (60 mL)

Tangy Tomato Salad

A great salad to take along for a picnic or to serve at a barbecue.

10		Roma tomatoes, coarsely chopped	10	
1		medium yellow bell pepper, cut in julienne slices	1	
1		medium red onion, cut in thin slices, then cut in half and rings separated	1	
1		jalapeño pepper, finely chopped	1	
1	tbsp.	olive oil	15	mL
1		lemon, juice of (3 tbsp. or 45 mL)	1	
1	tsp.	ground cumin	5	mL
1/2	tsp.	paprika	2	mL
2	tbsp.	finely chopped fresh parsley	30	mL
2		garlic cloves, minced	2	

In a medium bowl, combine tomatoes, yellow pepper, onion, and jalapeño pepper.

In a small bowl or measuring cup, stir together olive oil, lemon juice, cumin, paprika, parsley and garlic. Pour over salad and stir to combine. Let sit for about 30 minutes before serving to allow flavors to blend.

Serves 6.

Pictured opposite.

Salads

Clockwise from front lefthand side:

Bueno Broccoli Salad, page 68

Rice and Red Bean Salad, page 75

Tangy Tomato Salad, page 70

Black Bean Salad

1		medium green bell pepper, chopped	1	
1		medium red bell pepper, chopped	1	
1		jalapeño pepper, finely chopped	1	
2		large tomatoes, diced	2	
½		large red onion, chopped	½	
19	oz.	can black beans, drained and rinsed	540	mL
12	oz.	can whole-kernel corn, drained and rinsed	341	mL
2	tbsp.	vegetable oil	30	mL
¼	cup	lime juice	60	mL
2		garlic cloves, minced	2	
1	tsp.	ground coriander	5	mL
1	tsp.	ground cumin	5	mL
		black pepper, to taste		

In a large bowl, combine peppers, tomatoes, onion, black beans and corn.

In a small bowl, whisk together oil, lime juice, garlic, coriander, cumin and black pepper. Pour over vegetables and toss to coat. Serve immediately or refrigerate up to 24 hours, bringing to room temperature before serving.

Serves 8.

Spicy Four Bean Salad

Quick, nutritious and full of flavor!

2	cups	sliced green beans, cooked, drained and cooled	500	mL
19	oz.	can garbanzo beans, rinsed and drained	540	mL
14	oz.	can red kidney beans, rinsed and drained	398	mL
14	oz.	can black-eyed peas, rinsed and drained	398	mL
1		small red onion, cut in thin slices, then cut in quarters and rings separated	1	
1	cup	preserved salsa (at desired heat level – mild, medium or hot)	250	mL
1		lime, juice of, (1 to 2 tbsp. or 15 to 30 mL)	1	
		black pepper, to taste		

In a large bowl, combine green beans, garbanzo beans. kidney beans, black-eyed peas and onion. Stir in salsa, lime juice and black pepper to taste. Cover and refrigerate for at least 2 hours to allow flavors to blend.

Serves 6 to 8.

Garbanzo Beans

Also called chickpeas and ceci, these legume family members are popular in Indian, Middle Eastern, Spanish, Italian and Mexican dishes. Their mild nutty flavor and high-protein low-fat content have made them widely used n North and South America also. Used in soups, stews, salads and dips, garbanzos are widely available canned or dried.

Rice and Red Bean Salad

Pepper and Garlic Rice:

1	cup	vegetable stock	250	mL
1		small onion, chopped	1	
1		garlic clove, minced	1	
4-6		dashes hot pepper sauce	4-6	
1	cup	long-grain rice	250	mL
1¼	cups	water	310	mL

Lime and Wine Vinegar Dressing:

¼	cup	olive oil	60	mL
¼	cup	white wine vinegar	60	mL
1	tbsp.	lime juice	15	mL
1		garlic clove, minced	1	
1	tsp.	oregano	5	mL
¼	tsp.	dry mustard	1	mL
¼	tsp.	thyme	1	mL
½	tsp.	white sugar	2	mL
		black pepper, to taste		

Salad:

14	oz.	can red kidney beans, drained and rinsed	398	mL
½		large red bell pepper, chopped	½	
1		jalapeño pepper, seeded and finely chopped	1	

In a medium saucepan, combine stock, onion, garlic, hot pepper sauce, rice and water. Bring to a boil; cover and simmer for 20 minutes, or until liquid is fully absorbed.

To make salad dressing, in a small bowl, combine olive oil, vinegar, lime juice, garlic, oregano, dry mustard, thyme, sugar and black pepper.

In a medium bowl, combine rice, beans and peppers. Drizzle with salad dressing, and toss lightly to coat. Cover and chill.

Serves 6.

Pictured on page 71.

Thai Salad

Thai food is renowned for its fiery flavor combinations. Although we've never traveled to Thailand (yet!), we love the hot and spicy dishes we're able to enjoy in our local Thai restaurants and recreate at home.

Spinach Vermicelli Salad:

8	oz.	rice vermicelli*	250	g
2		carrots, grated	2	
2	cups	packed spinach leaves, cut in thin strips	500	mL
1		red bell pepper, cut lengthwise in quarters, seeded, then cut crosswise in 1/4" (1 cm) wide strips	1	

Ginger Lime Dressing:

1	3"	(8 cm) piece fresh ginger root, peeled and coarsely chopped	1	
1/4	cup	unsalted peanuts	60	mL
1/4	cup	water	60	mL
1		lime, juice of (1 to 2 tbsp. or 15 to 30 mL)	1	
2	tbsp.	low-sodium soy sauce	30	mL
2	tsp.	sugar	10	mL
2	tsp.	sesame oil	10	mL
1/2	tsp.	crushed red pepper flakes	2	mL
2	tbsp.	chopped fresh cilantro	30	mL

Cook vermicelli as per package directions. Drain and rinse under cold running water. Drain again and ensure all excess water is removed. Transfer vermicelli to a large bowl and add the carrot, spinach and red pepper strips. Toss to mix well.

In a food processor, add the ginger root and process until minced. Add the peanuts and process until finely chopped. Add water, lime juice, soy sauce, sugar, sesame oil and crushed red pepper; process to mix.

Pour dressing over the vermicelli mixture; toss to mix well. Sprinkle with chopped cilantro and serve.

Serves 6.

* Sometimes rice vermicelli comes in packages with no instructions or Chinese instructions only. To cook, soak rice vermicelli in hot water for 5 to 20 minutes, depending on thickness, until they are soft and pliable. Drain and rinse.

Fiesta Potato Salad

2	lbs.	red potatoes, peeled, cubed, cooked and cooled	1	kg
1½	cups	shredded low-fat Cheddar cheese	375	mL
1		medium red bell pepper, chopped	1	
14	oz.	can black beans, drained and rinsed	398	mL
1		celery stalk, thinly sliced	1	
1	cup	chopped jícama	250	mL
3		green onions, thinly sliced	3	
2	tbsp.	chopped fresh cilantro	30	mL
¾	cup	fat-free ranch salad dressing	175	mL
½	cup	salsa	125	mL

In a large bowl, combine potatoes, cheese, red pepper, black beans, celery, jícama, green onion and cilantro.

In a small bowl, stir together ranch dressing and salsa. Pour dressing over potato mixture and toss gently to coat.

Refrigerate for at least 1 hour before serving.

Serves 12.

Potatoes

Native to the Americas, potatoes were cultivated by the Incas thousands of years ago. Potatoes are classified as new or storage. New potatoes of any variety have not developed much starch, so they are best boiled. Mature, storage potatoes with a waxy texture, high moisture and low starch are boiling potatoes, e.g., round red or round white. The russet potato, elongated with a rough-textured skin has low moisture and high starch content, is best baked. Some potatoes, such as the long white potatoes, are all purpose. They can be roasted, boiled or baked. Specialty potatoes include the all-purpose Yukon Golden or Red Gold and the beautiful All Blue or Peruvian Purple which are respectively lilac blue and purple throughout.

Southwestern-Style Potato Salad

This spicy and flavorful potato salad is a refreshingly different addition to your backyard barbecue or picnic.

Chile Dijon Dressing:

1		garlic clove, minced	1	
2	tsp.	red chile powder	10	mL
¼	tsp.	ground cumin	1	mL
1	tsp.	Dijon mustard	5	mL
2	tbsp.	white wine vinegar	30	mL
3	tbsp.	olive oil	45	mL
		black pepper, to taste		

Salad:

8		large potatoes, peeled and cut in 1½" (4 cm) chunks (or 2 lbs. or 1 kg new potatoes)	8	
¼	cup	white wine vinegar	60	mL
1		medium red bell pepper, chopped	1	
1		medium green bell pepper, chopped	1	
6		green onions, chopped	6	
12	oz.	can whole-kernel corn, drained and rinsed	341	mL
½	cup	sliced black olives	125	mL
¼	cup	chopped fresh cilantro	60	mL

Combine the dressing ingredients by stirring together or shaking in a covered container. Set aside.

Cook potatoes until tender when pierced with a fork When potatoes are cooked, drain and cool for 10 minutes. Put cooled potatoes into a large bowl, and sprinkle with ¼ cup (60 mL) white wine vinegar. Stir gently. Add peppers, green onions, corn, olives and cilantro. Pour dressing over top and stir gently to combine.

Serves 8.

Fiesta Pasta Salad

Pasta Salad:

1½	cups	uncooked rotini pasta	375	mL
14	oz.	can red kidney beans, drained and rinsed	398	mL
12	oz.	can whole-kernel corn, drained and rinsed	341	mL
1		medium red bell pepper, chopped	1	
1		medium green bell pepper, chopped	1	
3		Roma tomatoes, chopped	3	
3		green onions, chopped	3	
¾	cup	shredded Cheddar cheese	175	mL

Herbed Tomato Dressing:

14	oz.	can diced tomatoes, undrained	398	mL
4	oz.	can chopped green chiles, drained	114	mL
3	tbsp.	olive oil	45	mL
2	tbsp.	red wine vinegar	30	mL
1		garlic clove, minced	1	
1	slice	onion, minced	1	slice
½	tsp.	oregano	2	mL
½	tsp.	dried basil	2	mL
1	tsp.	fresh parsley, minced	5	mL

Cook pasta in boiling water according to package instructions, or until firm to the bite. Drain well and allow to cool to room temperature.

Combine dressing ingredients in a small bowl and set aside.

When rotini has cooled, stir together all remaining salad ingredients in a large bowl. Stir dressing, pour over salad and toss to coat. Serve immediately.

Serves 4 as a main course or 8 as a side salad.

Southwestern Grilled Chicken Caesar Salad

Serve this delightful salad as a main course on one of those hot summer days!

Chile Worcestershire Marinade:

1	tbsp.	red chile powder	15	mL
2	tbsp.	Worcestershire sauce	30	mL
1	tsp.	ground cumin	5	mL
1/4	tsp.	black pepper	1	mL
1		garlic clove, minced	1	
1	lb.	skinless, boneless chicken breasts, cut into 1" (2.5 cm) wide strips	500	g

Chile Cumin Croutons:

2	tbsp.	olive oil	30	mL
1/2	tsp.	red chile powder	2	mL
1/2	tsp.	ground cumin	2	mL
1	pinch	cayenne pepper	1	pinch
6		thick slices of sourdough bread	6	

Roasted Garlic-Red Wine Vinegar Dressing:

1		head roasted garlic (see instructions on page 81)	1	
1	tsp.	anchovy paste	5	mL
1	tsp.	Dijon mustard	5	mL
1	tsp.	Worcestershire sauce	5	mL
2	tbsp.	olive oil	30	mL
2	tbsp.	red wine vinegar	30	mL
2	tsp.	Dijon mustard	10	mL
1/4	cup	grated low-fat Parmesan cheese	60	mL
1/4	cup	plain non-fat yogurt	60	mL
		black pepper, to taste		

Salad:

6	cups	torn romaine lettuce	1.5	L
2	cups	halved cherry tomatoes	500	mL

In a large plastic bag, add chile powder, Worcestershire sauce, cumin, black pepper and garlic. Mix well, then add chicken. Press out air and seal bag tightly. Massage bag to distribute marinade evenly. Refrigerate for at least 4 hours, turning and massaging bag occasionally.

continued

To make croutons, stir together olive oil, chile powder, cumin and cayenne in a small bowl. Brush over both sides of bread; cut into cubes and arrange in a single layer on a baking sheet. Toast in a preheated 350°F (180°C) oven, tossing once, for about 10 minutes or until crisp and golden. Let cool.

Add all dressing ingredients to a blender and blend together until smooth. Refrigerate for at least 1 hour to allow flavors to blend.

Preheat grill or broiler. Place chicken strips on grill or broiler pan that has been coated with nonstick cooking spray. Cook for 5 minutes on each side or until chicken is done.

In a large bowl, combine lettuce and tomatoes. Pour dressing over salad, add croutons and toss gently to coat.

Spoon salad onto serving plates, and top with chicken strips to serve.

Serves 4.

Roasted Garlic

Roasted garlic adds a wonderful rich, sweet flavor to dishes without adding any fat. Try it in mashed potatoes, sauces, dips, soups, appetizers and vegetable dishes.

To roast garlic, preheat oven to 350°F (180°C). Remove any of the skin that comes away easily and cut about 1/4" (1 cm) off the top of the garlic head. Place cut side up on a piece of foil, wrap and bake for 1 hour. Remove from oven and cool. To remove the garlic, turn the head upside down and gently squeeze the garlic out of the skins.

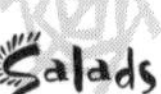

Fajita Salad

This delicious salad makes a perfect dinner on a hot, summer night.

Creamy Lime Dressing:

½	cup	fat-free sour cream	125	mL
½	cup	light mayonnaise	125	mL
⅓	cup	skim milk	75	mL
3	tbsp.	fresh lime juice	45	mL
1	tbsp.	balsamic vinegar	15	mL
2	tbsp.	chopped fresh cilantro	30	mL
2		garlic cloves, minced	2	

Spiced Chicken:

1	tbsp.	olive oil	15	mL
1	tsp.	red chile powder	5	mL
1	tsp.	ground cumin	5	mL
1	tsp.	paprika	5	mL
¼	tsp.	black pepper	1	mL
8	oz.	skinless, boneless chicken breast, cut into ½" (1.3 cm) strips	250	g

Salad:

2		heads romaine lettuce, washed, dried and torn in small pieces	2	
1		red bell pepper, cut lengthwise in quarters, seeded, then cut crosswise in ¼" (1 cm) wide strips	1	
1		small red onion, cut in thin slices, then cut in quarters and rings separated	1	
2		Roma tomatoes, each cut into 8 wedges	2	
½	cup	shredded reduced-fat Monterey Jack or Cheddar	125	mL
2	tbsp.	sliced ripe olives	30	mL
14	oz.	can pinto beans, rinsed and drained	398	mL

Combine all dressing ingredients until smooth. Cover and refrigerate.

Combine olive oil, chile powder, cumin, paprika and black pepper in a medium heavy-duty zip-top plastic bag. Add chicken and seal bag. Massage bag until chicken is thoroughly coated with the spice mixture.

Coat a large nonstick skillet with nonstick cooking spray. Heat over medium heat until skillet is hot and add chicken. Sauté for 8 to 10 minutes, or until chicken is done. Keep warm.

In a large bowl, combine all of the salad ingredients and toss to mix well. Divide salad ingredients among 6 plates and top each salad with the hot, cooked chicken. Drizzle with dressing and serve.

Serves 6.

Soups

Chilled Beet Soup with Spicy Cilantro Pesto

An elegant soup to serve for a special dinner.

Beet Soup:

4		medium beets, peeled and sliced	4	
1		medium onion, coarsely chopped	1	
1/4	cup	ginger root, peeled and coarsely chopped	60	mL
3		Roma tomatoes, coarsely chopped	3	
5	cups	cranberry juice	1.25	L
2	cups	water	500	mL

Spicy Cilantro Pesto:

1	cup	packed fresh cilantro leaves	250	mL
1		jalapeño pepper, seeded and sliced	1	
4		green onions, coarsely chopped	4	
1/2	cup	low-fat plain yogurt	125	mL
1	tbsp.	raspberry vinegar	15	mL

In a large stock pot, combine beets, onion, ginger root and tomatoes. Add cranberry juice and water. Bring to a boil, then lower heat to medium-low and simmer, covered, for about 1 hour, or until beets are very soft.

Process the soup, in batches, in a blender until smooth. Allow to cool, then cover and chill in the refrigerator.

To make Cilantro Pesto, in blender, purée cilantro, jalapeño, green onions, yogurt and vinegar until smooth.

Ladle the chilled soup into serving bowls. Drizzle swirls of cilantro pesto on the surface of the soup. If you desire a marbled design, drag the tip of a knife in lines across the surface of the soup in alternating directions.

Serves 8.

Pictured on page 89.

Fiery Chilled Soup

This unusual and light chilled soup makes a great starter to any summer dinner party.

1		large ripe cantaloupe, peeled and cut in large cubes	1	
1		cucumber, peeled, seeded and cut in large cubes	1	
1/4	cup	liquid honey	60	mL
1		fresh lime, grated rind	1	
1		fresh lime, juice of (1 to 2 tbsp. or 15 to 30 mL)	1	
1		jalapeño pepper, finely chopped	1	
1/2	tsp.	ground cumin	2	mL
2	cups	plain fat-free yogurt	500	mL
		grated lime rind, for garnish		

Combine cantaloupe and cucumber in a blender and blend until smooth. Pour half of the cantaloupe mixture into a medium bowl. To blender and remaining cantaloupe mixture, add honey, grated rind and juice of 1 fresh lime, jalapeño pepper, cumin and yogurt and blend until smooth. Add to cantaloupe mixture in bowl and mix well.

Cover and refrigerate for at least 4 hours to chill and to allow flavors to blend. Garnish with grated lime rind to serve.

Serves 6.

Chile Notes:

Fresh chiles will lose some heat and reconstituted dried chiles will get hotter when cooked.

Spicy Tomato Vegetable Soup

This soup is quick, spicy, healthy and delicious!

1	tsp.	olive oil	5	mL
1		large onion, chopped	1	
3		garlic cloves, minced	3	
1	cup	small pasta	250	mL
1 1/2	cups	salsa	375	mL
4	cups	tomato juice	1	L
28	oz.	can diced tomatoes, undrained	796	mL
1	tsp.	sugar	5	mL
1		medium zucchini, chopped	1	
3	cups	chopped fresh spinach	750	mL
		fresh parsley, for garnish		

In a large stock pot, heat oil over medium heat. Add onion and garlic and sauté until onion is translucent. Add pasta, salsa, tomato juice, tomatoes, sugar, zucchini and spinach; bring to a boil. Cover; reduce heat and simmer 20 minutes, or until pasta and zucchini are thoroughly cooked.

Garnish with fresh parsley to serve.

Serves 6.

Tomatoes

Related to potatoes and eggplant, as part of the nightshade family, tomatoes come in round and plum or pear shapes and in many sizes, from the tiny yellow pear tomato and cherry tomatoes to large beef-steak tomatoes. Sugars do not substantially increase once tomatoes are picked, so vine-ripened tomatoes are the most succulent. Red and green tomatoes used to be the only commercially available options. Now yellow and the sweeter gold and orange tomatoes are available. Store green to firm ripe tomatoes, unwrapped, at room temperature. Refrigerate fully ripe tomatoes on a shelf, not wrapped.

Roasted Red Pepper Soup

The licorice-flavored liqueur in this soup is a delightful complement to the roasted red peppers. Smooth and delicious, this is a lovely soup to serve for a special dinner party.

1	tbsp.	vegetable oil	15	mL
2		large onions, sliced	2	
2		garlic cloves, minced	2	
8		roasted red bell peppers (see page 58 for instructions)	8	
2	cups	chicken stock	500	mL
13½	oz.	can evaporated skim milk	385	mL
¼	cup	licorice-flavored liqueur (such as Sambuca)	60	mL
½	tsp.	cayenne pepper	2	mL
		black pepper, to taste		
1	tsp.	toasted fennel seed, for garnish (see page 112 for instructions)	5	mL

In a large stock pot, heat oil over medium heat. Add onions and garlic and sauté until onion is translucent. Add peppers and stock; simmer for 15 minutes.

In batches, purée the red pepper mixture in a blender until smooth. Transfer the red pepper mixture to a large saucepan and bring to a boil. Reduce heat and stir in the evaporated milk, liqueur, cayenne pepper and black pepper. Stir and continue cooking until heated through.

Garnish with toasted fennel seeds and serve immediately.

Serves 4.

Smoky Butternut Squash Soup

One of the things that we look forward to in winter (besides skiing!) is the warm pleasure that comfort foods bring us, pots of soup simmering on the stove and the smell of fresh bread cooking in the oven (or breadmaker these days!). This is a wonderful soup that is enhanced by the smoky, intense flavor of chipotle chile powder.

1	tbsp.	olive oil	15	mL
1		butternut squash, peeled and cubed	1	
2		medium onions, chopped	2	
1		large red bell pepper, chopped	1	
4		celery stalks, sliced	4	
2		poblano chiles, seeded and chopped	2	
2	tsp.	dried oregano	10	mL
1	tsp.	ground chipotle chile powder	5	mL
4	cups	vegetable stock	1	L
2	cups	frozen whole-kernel corn	500	mL
1		lime, juice of (1 to 2 tbsp. or 15 to 30 mL)	1	
3	tbsp.	finely chopped cilantro leaves	45	mL

In a large stock pot, heat oil over medium-high heat. Add squash, onions, red bell pepper, celery, poblano chiles, oregano and chipotle chile powder; sauté until onion is translucent. Add vegetable stock and corn and bring to a boil. Reduce heat and simmer 30 minutes, or until vegetables are tender. Stir in lime juice and cilantro and serve immediately.

Serves 4.

Chipotle Chiles

Chipotle chiles are ripened jalapeños that have been smoke-dried over peat. Chipotles are extremely hot and have a fabulous fruity-smoky flavor. For years a favorite in Mexico, this chile has taken the North American gastronomic world by storm. Chipotle is featured in everything including sauces, soups, salads, seasoning pastes, breads, etc.

Chilled Beet Soup with Spicy Cilantro Pesto, page 84

African Peanut Soup

The combination of peanuts and heat is apparently quite common in Africa. As my husband, Jim, is such a fan of both, I created this recipe for him after reading about this African flavor combination. Add some fresh bread and you have the perfect winter dinner.

2	tsp.	vegetable oil	10	mL
1		large onion, chopped	1	
3		garlic cloves, minced	3	
1		medium sweet potato, peeled and diced	1	
6	cups	vegetable stock	1.5	L
1	tsp.	dried thyme	5	mL
1/2	tsp.	ground cumin	2	mL
1/2	tsp.	cayenne pepper	2	mL
1/2	cup	uncooked long-grain rice	125	mL
1 1/2	cups	preserved salsa (mild, medium or hot, depending on taste preference)	375	mL
19	oz.	can garbanzo beans, drained and rinsed	540	mL
1		medium zucchini, diced	1	
1/2	cup	peanut butter (smooth or crunchy)	125	mL
2	tbsp.	chopped fresh parsley, for garnish	30	mL
2	tbsp.	chopped roasted peanuts, for garnish (optional)	30	mL

In a large stock pot, heat the oil over medium-high heat and sauté the onion, garlic and sweet potato, stirring frequently, until onion is translucent. Add the vegetable stock, thyme, cumin, cayenne pepper and rice and bring to a boil. Reduce heat and simmer for about 20 minutes, or until rice is cooked and vegetables are tender. Add the salsa, garbanzo beans and zucchini and cook for about 10 minutes, or until zucchini is tender. Add the peanut butter and stir until completely melted and combined. Serve garnished with the chopped parsley and peanuts, if desired.

Serves 6 to 8.

Curried Lentil Soup

This soup constitutes a hearty meal in itself or could be served over a bowl of rice. You're sure to enjoy these exotic and wonderful flavors.

1	tbsp.	olive oil	15	mL
1		large onion, chopped	1	
2		garlic cloves, minced	2	
1/2	cup	sliced celery	125	mL
1/2	cup	sliced carrot	125	mL
1		serrano or jalapeño pepper, finely chopped	1	
1	tbsp.	grated fresh ginger root	15	mL
1/2	tsp.	turmeric	2	mL
1/4	tsp.	cayenne pepper	1	mL
1/4	tsp.	cinnamon	1	mL
1/4	tsp.	allspice	1	mL
1/4	tsp.	ground coriander	1	mL
1/4	tsp.	ground cardamom	1	mL
3/4	cup	red lentils, rinsed and sorted	175	mL
28	oz.	can diced tomatoes, undrained	796	mL
8	cups	vegetable stock	2	L
19	oz.	can garbanzo beans, drained and rinsed	540	mL
3	tbsp.	lemon juice	45	mL
1/4	tsp.	black pepper	1	mL
1/4	cup	chopped fresh cilantro, for garnish	60	mL

Heat oil in a large stock pot over medium-high heat. Add onions and garlic and cook until onions are translucent. Add celery, carrots, serrano, ginger, turmeric, cayenne pepper, cinnamon, allspice, coriander and cardamom; cook for 2 minutes, or until spices become fragrant. Stir in lentils, tomatoes and vegetable stock and bring to a boil. Reduce heat and simmer for 20 minutes. Add garbanzo beans and continue to simmer for another 20 minutes. Stir in lemon juice and black pepper. Ladle into bowls and serve garnished with chopped fresh cilantro.

Serves 8.

Sopa de Lima

This soup is a favorite of mine. It's a great soup to prepare when you have a bunch of people around – get everyone chopping and filling the bowls with the ingredients. Pour on the stock and lime juice and it's ready to serve.

8	oz.	boneless, skinless chicken breasts	250	g
2	cups	water	500	mL
1		bay leaf	1	
1		small red onion, finely chopped	1	
3		Roma tomatoes, diced	3	
2-3		fresh serrano or jalapeño peppers, finely chopped	2-3	
1		medium avocado, peeled, seed removed and cubed	1	
1/4	cup	coarsely chopped fresh cilantro	60	mL
4	cups	chicken stock	1	L
1/4	cup	fresh lime juice	60	mL

In a medium saucepan, add the chicken, water and bay leaf and bring to a boil over high heat. Reduce heat and simmer chicken for 15 minutes, or until cooked through. Remove from heat and allow chicken to cool in the stock. When cool, drain and reserve stock. Shred the cooled chicken and set aside.

Heat reserved chicken stock plus an additional 4 cups (1 L) of stock in a medium saucepan. Divide the shredded chicken, onion, tomatoes, peppers, avocado and cilantro among 6 large soup bowls. Pour the heated chicken stock into each bowl over the chicken and vegetable mixture. Season with lime juice and serve immediately.

Serves 6.

Black Bean Soup

There are many variations of black bean soup and this is the one closest to our favorite from Puerto Vallarta.

1	lb.	dried black beans	500	g
4		dried chipotle chiles	4	
½	cup	water	125	mL
2	tbsp.	vegetable oil	30	mL
1		large onion, chopped	1	
3		garlic cloves, minced	3	
2		large carrots, chopped	2	
3		celery stalks, chopped	3	
1		large green bell pepper, chopped	1	
1		large red pepper, chopped	1	
4	cups	vegetable stock	1	L
1	cup	dry sherry	250	mL
2	tbsp.	honey	30	mL
2	tbsp.	ground cumin	30	mL
1	tbsp.	red chile powder	15	mL
1	tbsp.	dried oregano	15	mL
½	tsp.	ground cinnamon	2	mL
¼	tsp.	black pepper	1	mL
28	oz.	can diced tomatoes, undrained	796	mL
2		bay leaves	2	
8	tbsp.	fat-free sour cream, for garnish	120	mL
8		cilantro sprigs, for garnish	8	

Sort and wash the beans. Place beans in a large saucepan and cover with water to 2" (5 cm) above beans in the pot. Bring to a boil and cook for 3 minutes. Remove from heat; cover and let stand for 3 hours. Drain beans in a colander or sieve; set aside.

Place dried chipotles and ½ cup (125 mL) of water in a small saucepan and bring to a boil. Remove from heat, cover and let stand for 10 minutes. Place chipotle and water mixture in a food processor and process until smooth; set aside.

Heat oil in a large stock pot over medium-high heat. Add onion, garlic, carrots, celery, green pepper and red pepper and sauté for 8 minutes, or until vegetables are softened.

Add beans, chile purée, stock (be sure to rinse food processor bowl out with vegetable stock and add to the soup), sherry, honey, cumin, chile powder, oregano, cinnamon, black pepper, tomatoes and bay leaves; bring to a boil. Cover, reduce heat, and simmer for 1 hour. Discard bay leaves before serving.

Serve each bowl of soup garnished with a dollop of sour cream and a sprig of cilantro.

Serves 8.

Red Chile Powder

Red chiles have been eaten in the Americas for hundreds of years. In fact, Christopher Columbus wrote about chile in his diaries and said that "the people won't eat without it, for they find it very wholesome". Red chiles are dried and hung on "ristras" ("ristras" look like bananas growing on a tree), or are ground up into the powder that is featured in this recipe and many others throughout the book. Unlike the "chili powder" you find in your grocery store, pure ground red chile powder is uncut with anything and the flavor is unbelievably rich, hot and pure. Cayenne has been the usual term for hot, pure chile powder, but "red pepper powder" or "red chile powder" is now in more general use.

Chorizo and Garbanzo Bean Soup

8	oz.	chorizo sausage	250	g
1		large onion, chopped	1	
4		garlic cloves, minced	4	
2		large carrots, sliced	2	
2		celery stalks, sliced	2	
2		jalapeño peppers, thinly sliced	2	
1	tsp.	ground cumin	5	mL
½	tsp.	ground coriander	2	mL
½	tsp.	red chile powder	2	mL
¼	tsp.	black pepper	1	mL
28	oz.	can diced tomatoes, undrained	796	mL
19	oz.	can garbanzo beans, drained and rinsed	540	mL
4	cups	chicken broth	1	L
¼	cup	chopped fresh cilantro	60	mL

Remove casings from sausage and cut into slices (or use bulk chorizo if available). In a large stock pot, cook sausage, without stirring, for 5 minutes over medium heat. Drain off excess fat. Add onion, garlic, carrot and celery; cook, stirring often, for about 10 minutes, or until vegetables soften and sausage is thoroughly cooked.

Stir in jalapeño peppers, cumin, coriander, chile powder and black pepper. Cook, stirring constantly, for 1 minute. Add tomatoes and bring to a boil. Reduce heat and simmer, covered, for 10 minutes.

Stir in garbanzo beans, chicken broth and cilantro. Cover and simmer for 20 minutes.

Serves 8.

Chorizo

Garlic, chile powders and other spices are added to coarsely ground pork to make this zesty sausage. Traditional Mexican chorizo uses fresh pork; Spanish chorizo uses smoked pork while modern variations sometimes use ground beef, chicken or turkey. Chorizo adds rich spicy flavor to soups, stews, paella, quesadillas, enchiladas, even spicy pasta sauces.

Main Courses

Black Bean Salad Burritos

A great summer meal that is perfectly complemented with Fiesta Pasta Salad (see page 79), Jicama Mango Coleslaw (see page 69) or Spicy Four Bean Salad (see page 74).

Garlic Red Wine Vinegar Dressing:

1	tbsp.	olive oil	15	mL
1	tbsp.	red wine vinegar	15	mL
1/4	tsp.	oregano	1	mL
1/4	tsp.	dried basil	1	mL
1		garlic clove, minced	1	
		black pepper, to taste		

Black Bean Salad:

15	oz.	can black beans, drained and rinsed	425	mL
1/2		medium red bell pepper, chopped	1/2	
1/2		medium green bell pepper, chopped	1/2	
1		carrot, shredded	1	
2		green onions, chopped	2	
1/3	cup	salsa	75	mL
2		10" (25 cm) flour tortillas	2	
4		romaine lettuce leaves, washed and dried	4	

In a small bowl, whisk together dressing ingredients. Set aside.

In a medium bowl, combine beans, peppers, carrot, green onions and salsa. Add dressing and stir to combine ingredients.

Lay tortillas on a flat work surface. Spread half the bean mixture on each tortilla. Top with lettuce, and roll into a tube. Wrap in plastic wrap and refrigerate 2 to 4 hours. Slice each roll into 2 and serve.

Serves 4.

Veggie Fajitas

Balsamic Dijon Marinade:

1/4	cup	olive oil	60	mL
1/4	cup	balsamic vinegar	60	mL
2		garlic cloves, minced	2	
1	tbsp.	chopped parsley	15	mL
1	tsp.	Dijon mustard	5	mL
1/2	tsp.	dried basil	2	mL
		black pepper, to taste		

Veggie Fajitas:

1		medium red bell pepper, sliced in thin strips	1	
1		medium green bell pepper, sliced in thin strips	1	
1		medium yellow bell pepper, sliced in thin strips	1	
1		large onion, sliced in rings	1	
1		medium zucchini, sliced in thin rounds	1	
1	cup	broccoli florets	250	mL
12		8" (20 cm) flour tortillas	12	
		salsa		
		sour cream		
		Cheddar cheese, shredded		

In a small bowl, stir together all marinade ingredients. Set aside.

Prepare vegetables and place in a large bowl. Pour marinade over vegetables and stir to coat. Cover and refrigerate 2 to 4 hours, stirring occasionally.

Preheat barbecue. Place vegetables in a barbecue wok that has been coated with nonstick cooking spray. Grill vegetables over medium heat until tender-crisp, stirring frequently.

Serve grilled veggies in warmed tortillas with salsa, sour cream and Cheddar cheese.

Serves 4.

Spicy Black Bean Pie

15	oz.	can black beans, drained and rinsed	425	mL
1/2	cup	low-fat milk	125	mL
2		egg whites	2	
4	tbsp.	chopped fresh cilantro or parsley	60	mL
1	tsp.	vegetable oil	5	mL
1		large onion, chopped	1	
1		medium green bell pepper, chopped	1	
1		medium red bell pepper, chopped	1	
1/2	cup	vegetable stock	125	mL
2		garlic cloves, minced	2	
2x4	oz.	cans chopped green chiles, drained	2x114	mL
3	cups	tortilla chips, coarsely chopped	750	mL
1	cup	shredded light Cheddar cheese	250	mL

Preheat oven to 375°F (190°C).

In blender, process beans, milk, egg whites and 2 tbsp. (30 mL) of the cilantro or parsley until smooth. Set aside.

In a medium skillet, heat oil over medium heat. Add onion, peppers, vegetable stock, garlic and green chiles; cook for 5 minutes, stirring occasionally. Stir in remaining cilantro or parsley.

Place 1 1/2 cups (375 mL) of chopped tortilla chips in the bottom of a 2-quart (2 L) casserole. Pour bean mixture over chips. Spread vegetable mixture over bean mixture. Sprinkle with 1/2 cup (125 mL) of the cheese. Add remaining chips and top with remaining 1/2 cup (125 mL) of cheese.

Bake 30 to 35 minutes, or until cheese is golden brown. Serve with salsa, if desired.

Serves 6.

Great Bowls of Fire

This is a really quick vegetarian chili that is sure to warm you on those cold winter nights!

1	tsp.	olive oil	5	mL
1		medium onion, finely chopped	1	
6		garlic cloves, minced	6	
1	tbsp.	red chile powder	15	mL
1		reconstituted chipotle chile, minced (see page 111 for instructions)	1	
1/4	tsp.	black pepper	1	mL
2x15	oz.	cans black beans, drained and rinsed	2x425	mL
28	oz.	can diced tomatoes	796	mL
4	oz.	can chopped green chiles, drained	114	mL
		cilantro sprigs		

Heat oil in a large saucepan over medium-high heat. Add onion and garlic and sauté until onion is translucent. Add chile powder, chipotle, black pepper, black beans, tomatoes and green chiles. Stir and bring to a boil. Reduce heat and simmer 15 minutes.

Ladle chili into individual bowls and garnish with cilantro sprigs, if desired.

Serves 4.

Chile versus Chili

There are hundreds of varieties of chiles grown throughout the world. "Chile" is the Spanish spelling of the word, but you'll see it spelled differently wherever you travel. For example, in Australia and England the word is often spelled "chilli". Other variations are "chilie", "chillie", "chilley" and even "chilly" (which to me describes the temperature outside on a cool day!).

"Chili" is the name of a cooked dish, such as "chili con carne" or "chili verde" and doesn't refer to the chiles themselves.

Vegetarian Chili

More and more people are opting to select vegetarian dishes or to use meat as a condiment instead of the focus of every meal. To make this chili a complete dinner, try serving it as a topping for baked potatoes, over rice or with a crisp green salad and a crusty loaf of bread.

1	tbsp.	vegetable oil	15	mL
1		onion, coarsely chopped	1	
1		carrot, coarsely chopped	1	
2		jalapeño peppers, finely chopped	2	
2	tbsp.	red chile powder	30	mL
1		medium red bell pepper, chopped	1	
1		medium green bell pepper, chopped	1	
2		celery stalks, sliced	2	
1		medium zucchini, cubed	1	
3		garlic cloves, minced	3	
1	tsp.	dried oregano	5	mL
1	tsp.	dried basil	5	mL
2	tsp.	ground cumin	10	mL
12	oz.	dark beer, such as porter or stout	341	mL
1	tbsp.	grated unsweetened chocolate	15	mL
1	tsp.	sugar	5	mL
2		bay leaves	2	
28	oz.	can diced tomatoes, undrained	796	mL
19	oz.	can black beans, drained and rinsed	540	mL
19	oz.	can white kidney beans, drained and rinsed	540	mL
10	oz.	can whole-kernel corn, undrained	300	mL
		fat-free plain yogurt, chopped green onions and/or grated Cheddar cheese, for garnish (optional)		

In a large stockpot, heat oil over medium heat. Add onion, carrot, jalapeño and chile powder; cook until vegetables are softened, about 8 minutes, stirring frequently.

Stir in bell peppers, celery, zucchini, garlic, oregano, basil and cumin. Cook for 3 minutes, stirring frequently. Pour in beer; bring to a simmer and cook for 10 minutes.

Stir in chocolate, sugar, bay leaves, tomatoes, beans and corn. Bring to a boil; reduce heat to low; cover and simmer for 30 minutes.

Remove bay leaves and serve. May be garnished with fat-free plain yogurt, chopped green onions and/or grated Cheddar cheese.

Serves 6.

Pesto Pizza

This pizza makes a great dinner when you're in a rush; great flavor with little fuss.

Cilantro Pesto:

2		garlic cloves, peeled	2	
2	cups	cilantro leaves, packed	500	mL
1	tbsp.	pine nuts, toasted	15	mL
1	tbsp.	olive oil	15	mL
2	tbsp.	lime, juice of	30	mL
2	tbsp.	grated Parmesan cheese	30	mL
		black pepper, to taste		
1/4	cup	V-8 juice	60	mL

Pizza:

1		large seasoned Italian flat bread	1	
4		roasted red bell peppers, cut in strips (see page 58 for roasting instructions)	4	
1	cup	shredded Monterey Jack cheese	250	mL
		fresh cilantro sprigs, for garnish		

Preheat oven to 425°F (220°C).

To make pesto, place garlic in food processor and pulse until minced. Add cilantro leaves, pine nuts, olive oil, lime juice, Parmesan cheese and black pepper; pulse until finely chopped. While processor is running, gradually add V-8 juice and process until smooth.

Place seasoned Italian flat bread on pizza pan and spread pesto evenly to within a 1/2" (1.3 cm) of the outside edge. Top with red pepper strips and sprinkle with Monterey Jack cheese.

Bake for 15 minutes, or until cheese is bubbly. Garnish with fresh cilantro. Cut into wedges to serve.

Serves 4.

Southwestern Pizza

Another pizza recipe for you to try on a rushed weeknight or on Friday after a long week.

1	tsp.	olive oil	5	mL
½		onion, chopped	½	
1		garlic clove, minced	1	
15	oz.	can black beans, drained, rinsed and coarsely mashed	425	mL
1	tbsp.	red chile powder	15	mL
1		prebaked whole-wheat pizza crust	1	
½		medium red bell pepper, chopped	½	
½		medium green bell pepper, chopped	½	
½	cup	frozen corn, thawed	125	mL
1	cup	salsa	250	mL
½	cup	shredded Monterey Jack cheese	125	mL

Preheat oven to 375°F (190°C).

Heat oil in a medium nonstick skillet over medium heat. Add onion and garlic and sauté until onion is translucent. Add beans and chile powder and heat through.

Spread pizza crust with bean mixture, then sprinkle with peppers and corn. Drizzle salsa over and top with cheese.

Bake 20 minutes, or until heated through and cheese is melted and bubbling.

Serves 4 (2 slices each).

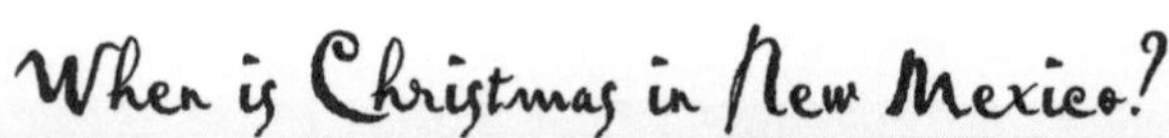

Christmas in New Mexico is when you go to a restaurant and they ask if you want red or green chile sauces with your order of enchiladas or burritos. If you can't make up your mind, just order "Christmas" and you'll get a taste of both sauces with your meal.

New Mexicans will tell you that there are only 2 seasons in their state: red and green – referring to the 2 basic kinds of chiles!

Linguine with Roasted Red Peppers and Capers

Jim and I adore pasta dishes and this is one of our favorites.

1	lb.	linguine	500	g
2	tbsp.	olive oil	30	mL
4		garlic cloves, minced	4	
1/4	tsp.	crushed red pepper flakes	1	mL
4		roasted red peppers, chopped (see page 58 for instructions)	4	
4	tbsp.	pickled capers, drained	60	mL
		black pepper, to taste		
1/2	cup	feta cheese, crumbled	125	mL

Cook linguine in boiling water according to package directions or until firm to the bite.

Meanwhile, in a large nonstick skillet, heat oil over medium heat. Add garlic and crushed red pepper, and cook for about 30 seconds, stirring constantly, until fragrant but not browned. Remove from heat and add roasted red peppers and capers. Season with black pepper to taste.

Reserve 1 cup (250 mL) of the pasta water. Drain linguine and add to the roasted red pepper mixture. Return skillet to the heat; mix in reserved pasta water and heat thoroughly, stirring constantly.

Transfer pasta mixture to serving dish and sprinkle with feta cheese. Serve immediately.

Serves 4.

Capers

Capers are the unopened flower bud of a bush that grows in the Mediterranean. Contrary to popular belief, they are in no way related to fish! They are usually packed in brine, so they should be rinsed before using. Select small capers and try them in everything from salads, pasta dishes, with smoked salmon or other fish dishes, in egg salad sandwiches and devilled eggs, in vegetables, sauces to pizza!

Pasta Azteca

This recipe was inspired by the description of a featured dish from a restaurant in Puerto Vallarta in a tourism magazine. Jim and I never got there to try the dish before leaving, but the description sounded so enticing that it haunted me until I developed this recipe.

Cilantro Pesto:

3		garlic cloves, peeled	3	
2	cups	cilantro leaves, packed	500	mL
2	tbsp.	toasted pine nuts (see page 141 for instructions)	30	mL
1		lime, juice of (1 to 2 tbsp. or 15 to 30 mL)	1	
2	tbsp.	grated Parmesan cheese	30	mL
		black pepper, to taste		
¼	cup	olive oil	60	mL

Pasta:

12	oz.	linguine or rotini pasta	341	mL
¼	cup	sun-dried tomatoes	60	mL
1	tbsp.	olive oil	15	mL
2		garlic cloves, minced	2	
1		small red onion, cut in thin slices, then cut in quarters and rings separated	1	
½	cup	fresh mushrooms, sliced (see page 170)	125	mL
1	cup	corn kernels (cut from cob or thawed fresh-frozen kernels)	250	mL
1		medium red pepper, cut in julienne slices	1	
1		small jícama, cut in julienne slices	1	
1	tbsp.	toasted pine nuts	15	mL

In a food processor, process 3 garlic cloves until minced. Add cilantro leaves, 2 tbsp. (30 mL) toasted pine nuts, lime juice, Parmesan cheese and black pepper. While processor is running, slowly add olive oil. Pesto may be covered and kept in refrigerator for 2 to 3 days.

Cook pasta in boiling water according to package directions, or until firm to the bite. Drain and place in serving bowl.To reconstitute tomatoes, pour boiling water over them and let soak for 15 minutes. Drain, then chop.

In a large nonstick skillet, heat oil over medium-high heat. Sauté garlic, red onion and mushrooms until just tender, about 5 to 8 minutes. Add corn, red pepper, jícama and reconstituted sun-dried tomatoes; sauté for 2 minutes. Add to pasta along with pesto and toss well. Sprinkle with 1 tbsp. (15 mL) of toasted pine nuts before serving.

Serves 6.

Pictured opposite.

Pasta Azteca, page 106

Szechuan Noodles with Spicy Peanut Sauce

My husband, Jim, is absolutely crazy about peanut butter. He loves this pasta dish that is inspired by the cuisine of the Szechuan province in China. Try it with the Perky Pepper Stir-Fry featured on page 129 and rice.

1/3	cup	peanut butter	75	mL
1/2	cup	boiling water	125	mL
1/4	cup	rice vinegar	60	mL
4		green onions, chopped	4	
2		garlic cloves, minced	2	
2	tbsp.	sodium-reduced soy sauce	30	mL
1/2	tsp.	crushed red pepper flakes	2	mL
1	lb.	soba noodles*	500	g

In a small bowl, mix peanut butter with boiling water until smooth. Stir in green onions, garlic, vinegar, soy sauce and red pepper flakes and combine until smooth. Set aside.

In a large pot of boiling water, cook noodles until just tender, as per package directions. Drain the noodles and transfer them to a serving bowl. Pour on the peanut sauce and toss to thoroughly coat the noodles. Serve immediately.

Serves 4.

*Soba noodles are brownish-gray Japanese noodles that are made with buckwheat flour.

Chile Air Conditioning

In addition to their use in Mexican food, chiles are also used extensively in other cultures' cuisines such as Thai, Hunan, Szechuan, East Indian and African. Most hot food originates in countries with hot climates (I always say that we need the hot foods in our colder climates to stay warm, from the inside out!). One of the likely reasons for this is that spice was probably used to mask spoiled food when refrigeration wasn't yet available. Another reason is that eating hot food creates perspiration, which creates an "air-conditioning" system when air evaporates the moisture on skin and garments.

Grilled Tequila Salmon Steaks

This decadent marinade will keep your salmon moist and give it a real kick. This marinade will work well on any other firm fish steak or fillet as well.

3		fresh limes, peels grated	3	
½	cup	fresh lime juice	125	mL
⅓	cup	tequila	75	mL
¼	cup	olive oil	60	mL
2		jalapeño peppers, seeded and finely chopped	2	
2	tsp.	sugar	10	mL
2	tsp.	green chile powder	10	mL
4		large salmon steaks	4	

Place grated lime peel in a small bowl and add ½ cup (125 mL) of fresh lime juice. Add tequila, olive oil, jalapeños, sugar and chile powder; stir well.

Place salmon in a medium heavy-duty zip-top plastic bag. Pour marinade mixture and seal bag. Massage bag until salmon is thoroughly coated with marinade. Refrigerate 4 hours or overnight, massaging bag and mixture occasionally.

Lightly oil barbecue grill and preheat to medium. Remove salmon from bag and place directly onto the hot grill. Cook with lid closed for 8 minutes per side, or until salmon is done.

While salmon is grilling, pour remaining marinade into a small saucepan and bring to a boil. Continue to boil, uncovered, until mixture is reduced by half, at least 3 minutes. Pour sauce over salmon steaks on serving plate.

Serves 4.

Green Chiles

A green chile is just an unripened chile which will eventually turn red, orange or purple, depending on the variety. Fresh green chiles are only available for a few months each summer, usually starting in late July. Green chiles have a wonderful flavor that is perhaps best experienced when they are roasted (especially over an open flame) and then peeled or else ground as a powder. Green chile cuisine has been developed in New Mexico and is only about a century old.

Chipotle Marinated Chicken

4		garlic cloves	4	
2		chipotle chiles, reconstituted and drained (see instructions below)	2	
1/4	cup	fresh cilantro	60	mL
2	tbsp.	honey	30	mL
3	tbsp.	vegetable oil	45	mL
2	tbsp.	balsamic vinegar	30	mL
1		lime, juice of (1 to 2 tbsp. or 15 to 30 mL)	1	
1/2	tsp.	ground cumin	2	mL
		black pepper, to taste		
6		boneless, skinless chicken breasts	6	

In a food processor, process garlic until minced. Add chipotle chiles and process until minced. Add cilantro, honey, vegetable oil, balsamic vinegar, lime juice, cumin, and black pepper; process until smooth. Pour over chicken; cover and refrigerate several hours or overnight (chicken may be marinated in a plastic bag as well).

Preheat barbecue and grill chicken over medium-high heat, about 8 minutes on each side, or until no longer pink in center.

Serves 6.

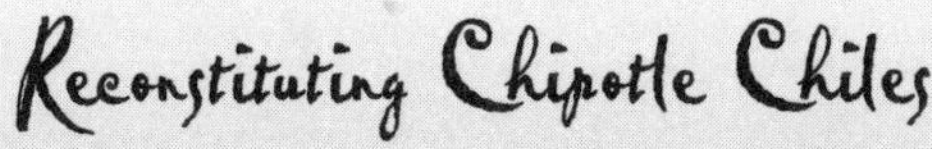

To reconstitute chipotle chiles, simply cover them in boiling water and soak them for approximately 1 hour. If whole dried chipotles aren't available, 2 canned chipotles in adobo sauce or 2 tsp. (10 mL) of ground chipotle powder may be substituted.

Cumin Chicken with Salsa

1		small tomato, chopped	1	
1/2		small cucumber, chopped	1/2	
1/2		medium green bell pepper, chopped	1/2	
1		jalapeño pepper, finely chopped	1	
2	slices	red onion, chopped	2	slices
1	tbsp.	ground cumin, toasted (see below for instructions)	15	mL
1	tsp.	black pepper	5	mL
4		boneless, skinless chicken breasts	4	
1	tbsp.	vegetable oil	15	mL
1	tbsp.	red wine vinegar	15	mL

In a small bowl, stir together tomato, cucumber, peppers and onion; set aside.

In a small bowl, stir together cumin and black pepper. Rub into both sides of each chicken breast.

Heat oil in a large nonstick skillet over medium-high heat. Add chicken and cook approximately 7 minutes per side, or until done. Remove chicken to serving plate; cover and keep warm.

Add vinegar to skillet and cook for 2 minutes, stirring constantly. Pour over tomato mixture and stir to combine. Serve chicken with salsa on the side.

Serves 4.

Toasting Spices

Toasting spices is a technique used to deepen and intensify the flavors of spices. Spices take on enhanced flavor when exposed to heat.

To toast dry spices, heat a small nonstick skillet over medium heat for 1 minute. Place whole or ground spices in skillet and stir until very fragrant and the color begins to deepen (be very careful not to overcook or burn). Remove from heat and cool. If using seeds, use a mortar and pestle or coffee grinder to grind into powder. I generally only toast the spices that I need immediately as the intensity of the flavor diminishes after about 1 week.

Grilled Chicken with Avocado Salsa

Avocado Salsa:

2		ripe avocados, chopped	2	
2		tomatoes, chopped	2	
1		small red onion, chopped	1	
1		jalapeño pepper, finely chopped	1	
1		lime, juice of	1	
1	tbsp.	olive oil	15	mL

Grilled Chicken:

1/4	cup	vegetable oil	60	mL
2	tsp.	ground cumin, toasted (see page 112 for instructions)	10	mL
1	tsp.	chopped cilantro	5	mL
2	tbsp.	liquid honey	30	mL
1		lime, juice of	1	
		black pepper, to taste		
4		boneless, skinless chicken breasts, halved	4	

In a small bowl, stir together the salsa ingredients. Salsa can be made up to 4 hours in advance and refrigerated until ready to serve.

In a medium bowl, combine vegetable oil, cumin, cilantro, honey, lime juice and black pepper. Add chicken to the marinade, and marinate for at least 4 hours or overnight.

Grill the chicken and serve it with the salsa.

Serves 4.

Hot Preferences

Chiles are the second most common spice in the world, following salt.

Jalapeño Pepper Jelly Glazed Chicken Breasts

Wondering how to use up that opened jar of jalapeño pepper jelly sitting in your refrigerator? Then you'll love this easy and delicious dinner idea which is beautifully complemented with steamed rice!

3	tbsp.	jalapeño pepper jelly	45	mL
1	tsp.	Dijon mustard	5	mL
1	tbsp.	lime juice	15	mL
4		boneless, skinless chicken breast halves	4	
		black pepper, to taste		
1	tbsp.	vegetable oil	15	mL
2		carrots, cut in 2" (5 cm) julienne strips	2	
2		celery stalks, cut in 2" (5 cm) julienne strips	2	
1	tbsp.	fresh parsley sprigs, for garnish	15	mL

In a small bowl, combine jelly, mustard and lime juice; set aside.

Season both sides of the chicken breasts with black pepper.

In a large nonstick skillet, heat oil over medium-high heat. Add chicken breasts and cook, turning once, until browned, about 4 minutes per side.

Push the chicken to one side, add the carrot and celery strips and cook for 1 minute, stirring constantly. Add the jelly mixture, and stir to coat the chicken. Cook until the sauce is reduced to a glaze, about 30 seconds. Season with black pepper.

Transfer the chicken to a serving platter and spoon the carrots and celery on top. Garnish with parsley and serve.

Serves 4.

Jamaican Jerk Chicken

Jim and I travelled to Jamaica on our first trip abroad (more years ago than I care to admit!) and have fabulous memories of a place called "The Pork Pit" in Montego Bay. We went there several evenings, picked up some jerk chicken and created a picnic for ourselves on the beach with fresh bread, fruits and vegetables that we found in the market. Oh yes, and some Red Stripe beer, as well!

Jerk Marinade:

1		medium onion, cut in quarters	1	
1		habañero pepper	1	
3		garlic cloves, peeled	3	
6		green onions, coarsely chopped	6	
1/4	cup	sodium-reduced soy sauce	60	mL
1/4	cup	orange juice	60	mL
1	tbsp.	vegetable oil	15	mL
1	tbsp.	red wine vinegar	15	mL
1	tsp.	ground allspice	5	mL
1/2	tsp.	dried thyme	2	mL
1/4	tsp.	ground mace	1	mL
1/4	tsp.	ground nutmeg	1	mL
1/4	tsp.	ground cinnamon	1	mL
1/4	tsp.	curry powder	1	mL
1/4	tsp.	black pepper	1	mL
6		boneless, skinless chicken breasts	6	

Add onion, habañero pepper, garlic and green onions to food processor and process until puréed. Add next 11 ingredients (to black pepper) and process to mix.

Place chicken in a large heavy-duty zip-top plastic bag. Pour in jerk marinade and seal bag. Massage bag until chicken is thoroughly coated. Refrigerate for a minimum of 4 hours or overnight to allow flavors to blend, massaging bag and ingredients occasionally.

Grill over high heat for about 20 minutes on each side or bake at 325°F (160°C) for 40 to 45 minutes, or until chicken is done and there is no remaining pink color inside meat.

Serves 6.

Chicken and Vegetable Curry

While doing a book signing in Calgary, I met a wonderful couple that market the most amazing masala. It inspired me to try cooking some East Indian dishes. Thanks to Naazima and Tim, Jim and I have grown to love this cuisine and we absolutely adore their "Sultana Ali Homemade Magic Curry Powder" (please contact me if you'd like to find out how to order their fabulous product).

2	tbsp.	masala or blended curry powder	30	mL
2	tsp.	paprika	10	mL
1	tbsp.	red chile powder	15	mL
		water, to make paste		
1	tbsp.	vegetable oil	15	mL
1		onion, chopped	1	
3		garlic cloves, minced	3	
6		boneless, skinless chicken breasts, cut into 2" (5 cm) chunks	6	
2		jalapeño peppers or serrano chiles, finely chopped	2	
1	tsp.	fresh lemon juice	5	mL
2		potatoes, peeled and cut in 1" (2.5 cm) chunks	2	
		water		
2		carrots, peeled and sliced	2	
19	oz.	can chickpeas, drained and rinsed	540	mL
1/2	cup	chopped fresh cilantro	125	mL

In a small bowl, mix together masala, paprika, chile powder and enough water to make a smooth paste.

In a large skillet, heat oil over medium-high heat. Add onion, garlic and chicken and cook until evenly browned. Lower heat to medium and add curry mixture and jalapeño pepper. Stir mixture constantly for 2 to 3 minutes. Add lemon juice.

Add potatoes and enough water to cover mixture in skillet. Bring to a boil and cook, covered, for 10 minutes. Add carrots and chickpeas and cook, covered, for 30 minutes longer. Taste and adjust seasonings if necessary. Transfer to serving dish and sprinkle with cilantro.

Serves 6.

Variations: This recipe can be prepared with beef or pork instead of chicken or, if you'd prefer a vegetarian version, eliminate the meat completely. For a vegetarian version, you may want to add a head of cauliflower florets when you add the carrots.

Chili Verde Burritos

1	tsp.	dried oregano	5	mL
1	cup	water	250	mL
1½	lbs.	tomatillos, husked and rinsed (see page 153 for information and instructions)	750	g
4		garlic cloves, peeled	4	
2		jalapeño peppers, ends removed and halved	2	
2	tbsp.	vegetable oil	30	mL
1½	lbs.	pork tenderloin, cut into ½" (1.3 cm) cubes	750	g
1		medium onion, chopped	1	
2		garlic cloves, minced	2	
½	cup	finely chopped fresh cilantro	125	mL
		black pepper, to taste		
8		10" (25 cm) flour tortillas	8	

In a large nonstick saucepan, add oregano and toast over medium heat, stirring constantly, until fragrant but not browned. Add water, tomatillos, garlic and jalapeño peppers; bring to a boil over medium-high heat. Reduce heat to medium, cover and cook until tomatillos are tender, about 15 minutes. Cool tomatillo mixture and coarsely purée in blender in small batches.

Heat oil in a large skillet over medium-high heat. Add pork, onion and garlic; sauté for 10 minutes. Reduce heat to medium-low. Add tomatillo sauce and cilantro, and simmer until pork is tender and sauce thickens, stirring occasionally, about 30 minutes. Season with black pepper to taste.

Meanwhile, stack tortillas and wrap in foil. Bake in a preheated 350°F (180°C) oven until warm, about 10 minutes.

Place tortillas on a flat work surface. Divide pork mixture evenly among the tortillas. Fold in 2 sides, then roll up from bottom. Arrange seam side down on serving plates.

Serves 4.

Chimichurri Flank Steak

Although chimichurri, a spicy Argentine red pepper garlic sauce, is delicious when served with any grilled meat, this recipe turns an inexpensive lean steak into a Latin American flavor adventure!

1½	lbs.	flank steak	750	g
1		recipe for Chimichurri (see page 150)	1	

Trim any fat from the flank steak and discard the fat. Score surface of the steak about ⅛" (3 mm) deep and 2" (5 cm) apart. Place steak in a resealable plastic bag or in a shallow dish. Pour half of the prepared chimichurri over the steak and coat the steak evenly with the sauce. Press out any air and tightly seal the bag or cover the dish. Let stand at room temperature, turning once, for 30 minutes or refrigerate overnight. Place remaining chimichurri in an airtight container and refrigerate until ready to serve.

When ready to cook steak, grease grill and preheat barbecue. Place steak with chimichurri coating directly on the grill, close lid and cook over high heat until seared and browned, turning once (8 to 10 minutes per side for medium-rare, 10 to 13 minutes for medium). Cooking flank steak beyond medium will toughen it.

Transfer steak to a cutting board and cover with foil. Let stand for 5 minutes. Using a very sharp knife, cut diagonally across the grain into very thin slices. Slice the entire steak as flank steak tends to toughen as it stands. Serve immediately with reserved chimichurri as a condiment.

Leftover steak will keep well, covered and refrigerated, for up to 2 days.

Serves 4 to 6.

That's a Wrap!

Spread 2 tbsp. (30 mL) of left over Chimichurri on each 10" (25 cm) flour tortilla (1 per person). Arrange some left over beef down the center of the wrap and top with shredded lettuce, sprouts, grated carrot, chopped green onion, chopped radishes, etc.

Fold wrap up 2" (5 cm) from the bottom. Press gently to create a crease. Hold in place while folding left side of wrap over to cover filling.

Fold right side over to encase filling on all sides. Secure with a tester or wrap the bottom quarter in waxed paper or foil.

Pepper Steaks

A new twist on an old favorite!

1	tsp.	red chile powder	5	mL
1/2	tsp.	garlic powder	2	mL
1/2	tsp.	black pepper	2	mL
1/2	tsp.	dried oregano	2	mL
1/2	tsp.	ground cumin	2	mL
4	4 oz.	beef tenderloin steaks (about 1" [2.5 cm] thick), trimmed of fat	4x125	g
1	tsp.	vegetable oil	5	mL
1/2	cup	beef stock	125	mL
1/3	cup	balsamic vinegar	75	mL
3	tbsp.	jalapeño pepper jelly	45	mL

In a small bowl, combine chile powder, garlic powder, black pepper, oregano and cumin. Rub into both sides of the steaks.

In a large nonstick skillet over medium-high heat, heat oil. Add steaks and cook 4 minutes* on each side, or until cooked to desired doneness. Remove steaks from skillet; cover and keep warm.

To skillet, add beef stock, vinegar and jelly. Cook 5 minutes, or until slightly thickened, stirring frequently. Spoon sauce over steaks and serve.

Serves 4.

* Four minutes is for medium. Adjust time accordingly.

Marinated Sirloin Steaks

2		garlic cloves, peeled	2	
2		jalapeño peppers, cut in half lengthwise and stems and seeds removed	2	
2/3	cup	dry red wine	150	mL
1/3	cup	olive oil	75	mL
1/2	cup	fresh parsley sprigs	125	mL
1/2	tsp.	black pepper	2	mL
6		sirloin steaks	6	

In a food processor, process garlic until minced. Add peppers to food processor and process until finely chopped. Add wine, olive oil, parsley and black pepper; process until smooth.

Score surface of steaks about 1/8" (3 mm) deep and 2" (5 cm) apart. Place steaks in a large plastic bag and pour in marinade. Press out any air and seal tightly. Massage bag to distribute marinade evenly. Refrigerate overnight or at least 4 hours, turning and massaging bag occasionally.

Preheat grill to medium-high heat. Remove steaks from bag and grill, turning only once and brushing with the reserved marinade, until desired doneness is reached.

Serves 6.

Chile Heat

Contrary to popular belief, the seeds are not the hottest part of a chile. Rather, the greatest heat is found in the capsaicin oil, which is found in the membranes and near the stems of chile plants.

Vegetables & Side Dishes

Grilled Marinated Vegetables

My friend, Sheri, first introduced me to grilled marinated vegetables and Jim and I have enjoyed them often ever since. To make this dish a main course, serve over cooked pasta with the warmed marinade poured over.

Balsamic Dijon Marinade:

3	tbsp.	olive oil	45	mL
3	tbsp.	balsamic vinegar	45	mL
1	tbsp.	Dijon mustard	15	mL
2		garlic cloves, minced	2	
1	tbsp.	dried Italian seasoning	15	mL
½	tsp.	black pepper	2	mL
¼	tsp.	crushed red pepper flakes	1	mL

Vegetables:

1		small red onion, cut in quarters lengthwise, then cut in half across	1	
1		red bell pepper, cut in large chunks	1	
1		yellow bell pepper, cut in large chunks	1	
2		small zucchini, cut in 1" (2.5 cm) slices	2	
3		carrots, cut diagonally in thin slices	3	
12		asparagus spears, trimmed and cut diagonally in 1" (2.5 cm) pieces	12	
½	lb.	mushrooms, cleaned and cut in half	250	g

In a large heavy-duty zip-top plastic bag, mix together marinade ingredients and set aside. Prepare vegetables and add to marinade. Seal bag and toss to thoroughly coat. Allow to marinate for 30 minutes to allow flavors to blend, turning bag occasionally.

Preheat barbecue. Remove vegetables from bag, reserving marinade. Place vegetables in a barbecue wok or a wire grilling basket that has been coated with nonstick cooking spray. Place barbecue wok or grilling basket on grill rack and grill 8 minutes on each side, or until tender.

Place reserved marinade in a small saucepan and cook over medium heat until almost boiling. Pour warm marinade over grilled vegetables in serving dish.

Serves 6.

Colorful Cauliflower Medley

This medley may be served as a vegetable side dish or as a salad. Colorful and palate pleasing, it makes the perfect accompaniment to any meal, particularly on a warm summer evening.

1/4	cup	chopped fresh parsley	60	mL
1/3	cup	lemon juice	75	mL
2	tsp.	olive oil	10	mL
1		garlic clove, minced	1	
5	cups	cauliflower florets	1.25	L
2/3	cup	thinly sliced radishes	150	mL
2		jalapeño peppers, halved lengthwise, seeded, and thinly sliced	2	

In a small bowl, combine parsley, lemon juice, olive oil and garlic.

Steam cauliflower for 3 minutes, or until tender-crisp. Rinse under cold water and drain well.

In a medium bowl, combine cauliflower, radishes and jalapeños. Pour lemon juice mixture over top and toss to coat thoroughly.

Serves 6.

Cauliflower

This broccoli relative has a mild, nutty, slightly sweet cabbage-like flavor. Grey spots on the white florets are sun discolorations where the light penetrated the green leaves. Trim them off. Cauliflower heads should be compact and white with no black spots or loose florets. Store raw cauliflower, tightly wrapped in the refrigerator for up to 5 days; refrigerate cooked for up to 3 days. Lemon juice, 1 tbsp. (15 mL) in the cooking water, prevents discoloration. Cauliflower is a good source of vitamin C.

Mexican Vegetable Medley

1	tbsp.	olive oil	15	mL
4		carrots, cut in julienne slices	4	
2		chayote squash, cut in julienne slices	2	
2		zucchini, cut in julienne slices	2	
1		red bell pepper, cut into thin strips	1	
1		jalapeño pepper, minced	1	
2	tsp.	oregano, toasted (see page 112 for instructions)	10	mL
1	tbsp.	finely chopped fresh cilantro	15	mL
		black pepper, to taste		

Heat oil in a large nonstick skillet or wok over medium-high heat. Sauté the carrots for 2 minutes, stirring constantly. Add the chayote squash, zucchini, red pepper and jalapeño pepper, and sauté for about 5 minutes, stirring constantly.

Add oregano, cilantro and black pepper, and combine thoroughly. Serve immediately.

Serves 6.

Pictured opposite.

Chayote Squash

Chayote (pronounced cha-yó-tay), which is a relative of zucchini squash, is pear-shaped, light green in color and deeply creased in appearance. It can be found in most large supermarkets and is well worth searching for. When cooked, chayote retains its crispness. It is especially nice roasted or sautéed. Peel away the outer skin, slice in half and remove the thin pit. Then it's ready to slice and cook.

Vegetables & Side Dishes

Clockwise from lefthand side:

Mexican Vegetable Medley, page 124

Couscous with Black Beans and Corn, page 140

Madras Vegetables

A subtle taste of East Indian cuisine. Delicious!

1/2	tsp.	ground coriander	2	mL
1/2	tsp.	ground cumin	2	mL
1/2	tsp.	crushed red pepper flakes	2	mL
1/4	tsp.	dry mustard	1	mL
1/4	tsp.	ground ginger	1	mL
1/4	tsp.	ground turmeric	1	mL
2		garlic cloves, minced	2	
2	tbsp.	water	30	mL
2		tomatoes, diced	2	
1/2		large head of cauliflower, broken into florets	1/2	
1		zucchini, cubed	1	

In a large nonstick skillet over medium heat, combine spices, garlic, water and tomatoes. Stir together and cook for 5 minutes. Steam cauliflower and zucchini until tender crisp. Add to skillet and toss to coat with spice mixture. Serve immediately.

Serves 6.

Madras Curry

Madras curry powder tends to be hotter than the standard Indian curry. Curry powders are freshly ground blends of many spices and herbs including coriander, cumin, red chile peppers, black peppercorns, mustard seeds, turmeric, curry (or kari) leaves, fenugreek seeds, ginger, etc. Each family has a special blend that they prefer. Curry blends vary from region to region. Some blends also include cardamom, cinnamon, cloves, fennel, mace, nutmeg, poppy seeds, sesame seeds, saffron, tamarind, etc.,

Nuevo Vegetable Casserole

14	oz.	can tomato sauce	398	mL
2		garlic cloves, minced	2	
1	tbsp.	red chile powder	15	mL
1	tbsp.	white vinegar	15	mL
1	tsp.	ground cumin	5	mL
½	tsp.	crushed red pepper flakes	2	mL
12	oz.	can whole-kernel corn, drained	341	mL
3		medium zucchini, halved and sliced	3	
½		medium green bell pepper, chopped	½	
½		medium red bell pepper, chopped	½	
1	cup	shredded Cheddar cheese, divided	250	mL
½	cup	crushed baked tortilla chips	125	mL
4	oz.	can chopped green chiles	114	mL
½	cup	fat-free sour cream	125	mL
3		green onions, chopped	3	
1		medium tomato, chopped	1	

Preheat oven to 350°F (180°C).

In a medium saucepan over medium heat, combine tomato sauce, garlic, chile powder, vinegar, cumin and red pepper flakes. Bring to a boil, stirring frequently, then reduce heat to low and cook for 10 to 12 minutes. Set aside.

In a medium bowl, stir together corn, zucchini, peppers, ½ cup (125 mL) of the cheese, tortilla chips and green chiles. Spread the vegetable mixture in a 9 x 13" (23 x 33 cm) baking dish that has been coated with nonstick cooking spray.

Pour tomato sauce over casserole, and bake for 25 minutes. Sprinkle remaining ½ cup (125 mL) of cheese over top, and bake for 5 more minutes.

Remove casserole from oven; spread sour cream on top and sprinkle with green onions and tomato.

Serves 8.

Perky Pepper Stir-Fry

Try this quick and colorful stir-fry with the Szechuan Noodles with Spicy Peanut Sauce featured on page 109.

1		red bell pepper, cut in quarters lengthwise, seeded, then cut crosswise in 1/4" (1 cm) wide strips	1	
1		green bell pepper, prepared as above	1	
1		yellow bell pepper, prepared as above	1	
1		orange bell pepper, prepared as above	1	
1		serrano or jalapeño pepper, finely chopped	1	
2	tsp.	peanut oil	10	mL
3		garlic cloves, minced	3	
1/2	tsp.	sugar	2	mL

Prepare peppers and set aside.

Heat oil in a wok or large skillet over high heat. Add garlic and stir-fry until fragrant but not browned. Add peppers and stir-fry until just tender, or for about 2 to 3 minutes. Add sugar and stir-fry for another 30 seconds. Transfer to a heated serving dish and serve immediately.

Serves 4.

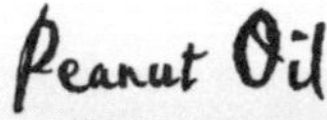

Peanut Oil

Cold-pressed peanut oil, usually found in Asian specialty markets, has a distinctive peanut flavor. North American peanut oil is not cold pressed and has a mild, light flavor. It is particularly valued for frying because of its high smoke point. Unlike other nut oils which have a very short shelf life, peanut oil keeps for a long time if stored in a cool dark place. People with peanut allergies are also violently allergic to peanut oil.

Sizzling Baked Onions

1	lb.	small boiling onions (about 1" [2.5 cm] diameter), peeled	500	g
1/4	cup	jalapeño pepper jelly	60	mL
1	tbsp.	brown sugar	15	mL
2	tbsp.	melted butter or margarine	30	mL

Preheat oven to 350°F (180°C).

Boil onions until tender, about 10 minutes. Drain.

Combine jelly, brown sugar and butter in a bowl. Add onions and stir to coat. Pour into a baking dish that has been coated with nonstick cooking spray, and bake for about 20 minutes, basting once during baking.

Serves 6.

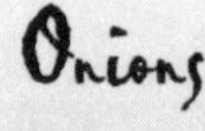

Onions

Onions are a fair source of Vitamin C. They are prized world wide for their distinctive pungent flavor which ranges from relatively mild to sharp. For no-tears onion chopping, chill onions before peeling or peel under running water and chop in the food processor. Store dried onions in a cool, dry place, in one layer if possible.

Stuffed Poblano Chiles

This vegetable dish has beautiful color and flavor. If poblano chiles aren't available in your local grocery store, green bell peppers may be substituted.

3		medium poblano chiles, cut in half lengthwise, seeded and membrane removed	3	
1		medium Roma tomato, finely chopped	1	
1/2	cup	frozen whole kernel corn, thawed	125	mL
1/2	cup	finely chopped red onion	125	mL
1/3	cup	grated Parmesan cheese	75	mL
1/4	cup	dry breadcrumbs	60	mL
1/4	cup	chopped fresh cilantro	60	mL
2	tbsp.	reduced-fat mayonnaise	30	mL
2	tbsp.	plain fat-free yogurt	30	mL
1	tsp.	red chile powder	5	mL
1/2	tsp.	black pepper	2	mL

Preheat oven to 375°F (190°C).

Prepare chiles.

In a medium bowl, combine tomato, corn, onion, cheese, breadcrumbs, cilantro, mayonnaise, yogurt, chile powder and black pepper. Divide vegetable mixture evenly among the chile halves and place on a baking sheet that has been coated with nonstick cooking spray. Bake for 20 minutes and serve immediately.

Serves 6.

Capsaicin Health Benefits

Capsaicin, the substance responsible for the heat in chile peppers, has been medicinally proven to protect against stomach ulcers and the ravages of alcohol. Really! Contrary to popular belief that ulcer sufferers should avoid spicy foods, a report published in "Digestive Diseases and Sciences" concluded that capsaicin increased blood flow in the stomach's mucous lining, which may help tissue healing. Chile also protects against the side effects of aspirin and chile eaters develop fewer peptic ulcers than those who eat plain food. Also, rates of stomach cancer are unusually low in countries where chile peppers are part of a regular diet as capsaicin appears to neutralize some carcinogens.

Swiss Chard with Spicy Chile Vinegar

Swiss chard was one of those special vegetables that Mom used to grow and we would enjoy for a very short period every summer when I was growing up. Mom never served Swiss chard with Spicy Chile Vinegar though!

2	lbs.	Swiss chard	1	kg
1/2		red bell pepper, cut lengthwise in quarters, then cut crosswise in 1/4" (1 cm) wide strips	1/2	
1/4	cup	water	60	mL
6	tbsp.	Spicy Chile Vinegar (see page 155 for recipe)	90	mL

Remove stems from the Swiss chard. Wash the leaves thoroughly and coarsely chop into 2" (5 cm) pieces. In a large stock pot, add Swiss chard, red pepper and water. Cover and cook over medium heat until tender, about 5 minutes. Drain thoroughly; add Spicy Chile Vinegar. Toss to coat and serve immediately.

Serves 6.

Variation: This recipe can be prepared using spinach if desired.

Swiss Chard

Also known as chard, this vegetable belongs to the beet family. The leaves can be prepared using spinach recipes; the stalks can be prepared using asparagus recipes. It is a good source of vitamins A and C and iron.

Baked Asparagus with Lemon-Mustard Sauce

Asparagus is a vegetable that I associate with spring in our northern climate. I've discovered that baking or roasting asparagus gives it a nutty flavor and it is much easier to prepare than traditional steaming.

1½	lbs.	fresh asparagus, washed, woody ends trimmed off (snap the ends off where they break naturally)	750	g
1	tsp.	vegetable oil	5	mL

Lemon-Mustard Sauce

1	tbsp.	fresh lemon juice	15	mL
2	tsp.	Dijon mustard	10	mL
1	tsp.	olive oil	5	mL
		black pepper, to taste		

Preheat oven to 450°F (230°C).

Place asparagus on a baking sheet that has been coated with nonstick baking spray. Drizzle with vegetable oil and toss to coat. Spread asparagus out in a single layer. Bake for 8 to 10 minutes, turning once, until tender-crisp.

While asparagus is baking, mix together lemon juice, Dijon mustard and olive oil. When asparagus is cooked, transfer to a serving dish and drizzle with the Lemon-Mustard Sauce. Season with pepper to taste.

Serves 6.

Spicy Baked Beets

These beets are really unusual and will hopefully make people feel more receptive to this underrated vegetable.

1	lb.	fresh small beets, scrubbed and tops and tails cut off	500	g
2		navel oranges, peeled and cut into 1/4" (1 cm) slices	2	
2	tbsp.	orange juice	30	mL
2	tbsp.	butter or margarine, melted	30	mL
1	tbsp.	prepared horseradish	15	mL
2	tsp.	fresh lime juice	10	mL
2	tsp.	grated ginger root	10	mL
1	tsp.	red chile powder	5	mL

Preheat oven to 350°F (180°C).

Place the beets in a glass casserole that has been coated with nonstick cooking spray and bake for 20 minutes, or until cooked through. Remove from oven and set them aside to cool.

When cooled, peel the beets and cut them into 1/4" (1 cm) slices. Arrange beets in a baking dish that has been coated with nonstick cooking spray and spread orange slices on top.

Mix the remaining ingredients together and pour over beets and oranges. Bake for 15 minutes, or until heated through.

Serves 6.

Green Beans with Dill and Pine Nuts

Green beans are a colorful and tasty addition to most dinners.

1	lb.	fresh green beans, trimmed and cut diagonally in 1" (2.5 cm) slices	500	g
1/4	cup	chopped fresh dill	60	mL
1	tbsp.	olive oil	15	mL
2	tsp.	fresh lemon juice	10	mL
2	tbsp.	toasted pine nuts (see page 141 for instructions)	30	mL
		black pepper, to taste		

Microwave or steam vegetables in a steamer basket for approximately 7 minutes, or until beans are tender-crisp. Drain thoroughly.

Add dill and olive oil; toss gently. Add lemon juice and black pepper to taste; toss again. Sprinkle with pine nuts to serve.

Makes 6 servings.

Dill

A Roman good luck symbol, dill is available fresh, dried and as dill seed. The feathery fronds of the dill plant are called dillweed and the fruit is dill seed. The distinctive aroma of fresh dill is destroyed by heat, so add dillweed just at the end of the cooking process. The flavor of the seeds is stronger than that of the dillweed.

Chile and Potato Gratin

2	cups	water	500	mL
12	oz.	can evaporated skim milk	341	mL
3		garlic cloves, minced	3	
1	tsp.	green chile powder	5	mL
½	tsp.	black pepper	2	mL
4		large potatoes, peeled and very thinly sliced crosswise	4	
1		medium onion, sliced very thinly	1	
2x4	oz.	cans chopped green chiles, undrained	2x114	mL

Preheat oven to 400°F (200°C).

In a medium bowl, combine the water, milk, garlic, chile powder and black pepper.

Spread the potatoes in a 9 x 13" (23 x 33 cm) baking dish that has been coated with nonstick cooking spray. Sprinkle onions and green chiles over potatoes and pour the liquid mixture over all, shaking the dish to settle the potatoes and liquid mixture in an even layer.

Bake for 45 minutes, or until potatoes are tender and the dish is bubbling and browned on top. Serve hot.

Serves 6.

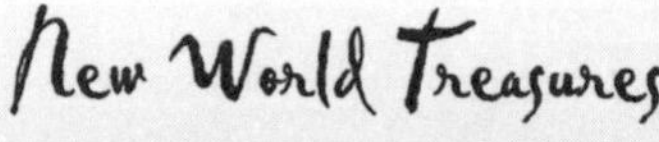

New World Treasures

Christopher Columbus discovered chiles (indigenous to the Americas) and brought them to Europe in 1492. Since then they have spread around the world to China, India, Malaysia, Indonesia, Africa, etc. It is hard to imagine the cuisines of many of these areas without the fiery, flavorful addition of chiles. These New World treasures proved to be longer lasting than the gold of the Americas.

Roasted Corn Succotash

I'm a real vegetable lover and this dish is a delightful addition to any meal. Practically a meal in itself!

3		ears fresh corn, kernels cut from cobs	3	
1		red bell pepper, chopped	1	
1		small onion, chopped	1	
1	tsp.	ground cumin	5	mL
1½	tbsp.	olive oil	22	mL
1		small zucchini, cubed	1	
2		garlic cloves, minced	2	
1		jalapeño, finely chopped	1	
½	cup	vegetable stock	125	mL
2	tbsp.	chopped fresh cilantro	30	mL
10	oz.	package frozen baby lima beans, thawed	284	g
⅛	tsp.	black pepper	0.5	mL
¼	tsp.	hot pepper sauce, or to taste	1	mL

Heat a large nonstick skillet over high heat. Add corn, red bell pepper, onion and cumin; sauté 5 minutes, or until vegetables are slightly blackened.

Reduce heat to medium-high. Add oil, zucchini, garlic and jalapeño; sauté for 2 minutes.

Add stock and remaining ingredients; cook for 2 minutes, or until thoroughly heated, stirring frequently.

Serves 6.

Chile Notes

Many red dyes are derived from chiles.

Corn on the Cob

You're probably wondering why I've included a page dedicated to corn on the cob. Most people boil the flavor and goodness out of corn and I thought it would beneficial to include some cooking alternatives and some fun toppings that I've found over the years. The late summer arrival of fresh corn is a big event in our area as I'm sure it is in yours and you'll want to try these alternative cooking methods to maximize corn's fabulous flavor.

Grilled Corn:

Soak unhusked corn in cold water for at least 1 hour. Grill unhusked corn over high heat, turning occasionally, for about 8 minutes, or until tender.

For a drier cob with a smokier flavor, husk corn that hasn't been soaked and grill over high heat, turning occasionally, for about 12 minutes, or until tender.

Microwaved Corn:

Place unhusked corn on a paper-towel-covered plate and microwave on high power: 7 minutes for 4 ears or 5 minutes for 2 ears.

Steamed Corn:

In a large pot with a steamer basket, bring 1 to 2" (2.5 to 5 cm) of water to a boil over high heat. Add husked corn to steamer basket, cover and steam for 5 to 7 minutes, or until tender.

Lime and Red Chile Topping:

Squeeze fresh lime juice over hot corn, sprinkle with red chile powder and black pepper. A very Mexican way to enjoy corn on the cob!

Oil of Olé:

Try brushing on some of the Oil of Olé, featured on page 154, with a pastry brush. Season with black pepper to taste and enjoy!

Toasted Garlic:

Separate the unpeeled cloves of a whole head of garlic. Toast garlic in a heavy skillet over medium heat, stirring often, for about 10 minutes, or until soft and partially blackened. Cool the garlic, peel and place in a small bowl. Mash the garlic with 1/2 tsp. (2 mL) of salt. Spread on hot corn.

Garlic-Lemon Vinaigrette:

In a small bowl, mix together 2 tsp. (10 mL) of olive oil, 1 tbsp. (15 mL) of fresh lemon juice, and 1 clove of minced garlic. Brush onto hot cobs of corn with a pastry brush.

Butter with Pepper:

If you can't give up butter on your corn on the cob, place 2 tbsp. (30 mL) of butter in a large, flat microwave dish. Sprinkle generously with black pepper, cover dish and microwave for 1 1/2 minutes on high, or until butter is melted. Add husked corn and roll in butter until thoroughly coated. Cover and microwave on high power: 7 minutes for 4 ears or 5 minutes for 2 ears.

Dried Chiles

When fresh chiles are dried they lose most of their vitamin C content, but their vitamin A content increases 100 times.

Couscous with Black Beans and Corn

$1\frac{1}{2}$	cups	water	375	mL
1	cup	uncooked couscous	250	mL
3	tbsp.	orange juice	45	mL
3	tbsp.	lemon juice	45	mL
1	tsp.	grated lemon rind	5	mL
1	tbsp.	olive oil	15	mL
$\frac{1}{4}$	tsp.	ground cumin	1	mL
$\frac{1}{8}$	tsp.	coarsely ground black pepper	0.5	mL
$\frac{1}{2}$	cup	cilantro leaves, chopped	125	mL
15	oz.	can black beans, rinsed and drained	425	mL
10	oz.	can whole-kernel corn, drained	285	mL
		cilantro sprigs for garnish (optional)		

Bring water to a boil in a medium-sized saucepan and stir in couscous. Remove from heat; cover and let stand 5 minutes. Fluff couscous with a fork.

While couscous is standing, combine orange juice, lemon juice, lemon rind, olive oil, cumin and black pepper. Stir to mix well.

Add cilantro, beans and corn to couscous and toss until well combined. Add orange juice mixture and mix well. Garnish with cilantro sprigs, if desired.

Serves 4.

Pictured on page 125.

Couscous

Couscous is a very fine-grained pasta made from semolina wheat. It is a staple food in the Middle East and has gained popularity around the world because of its versatility and quick preparation.

Saffron Rice with Toasted Pine Nuts

This delicious and exotic dish is the perfect accompaniment to the Chicken and Vegetable Curry featured on page 116 and the Madras Vegetables featured on page 127.

1	tbsp.	olive oil	15	mL
1		onion, chopped	1	
1		garlic clove, minced	1	
1	cup	long-grain rice, uncooked	250	mL
2	cups	water	500	mL
1/4	tsp.	salt (optional)	1	mL
1/4	tsp.	crushed saffron	1	mL
1/4	cup	toasted pine nuts	1	mL

In a large saucepan, heat oil over medium heat. Add onion and garlic; cook until onion is translucent. Add rice and cook, stirring often, for 5 minutes, or until rice is golden brown. Stir in water, salt (if using) and saffron. Increase heat to high and bring to a boil. Reduce heat to medium-low and simmer, covered, for 20 minutes, or until rice is tender and water has been absorbed.

Toast pine nuts in a small nonstick skillet over medium heat until lightly browned and fragrant. Be careful not to let them burn. Remove from heat and set aside.

Fluff rice with a fork and stir in toasted pine nuts. Serve immediately or, if making ahead, keep rice in oven on low heat for up to an hour before serving.

Serves 4.

Saffron

Have you ever wondered why saffron is so expensive? In fact, saffron is the world's most expensive spice because of its labor-intensive harvesting method. Saffron is the yellow-orange stigma of a small crocus which is predominantly found in southern Europe (Spanish saffron is perhaps the best known). Each crocus contains only 3 stigmas and they must be hand-picked and hand-dried. One ounce of saffron contains 14,000 stigmas! Fortunately, a tiny amount of saffron is sufficient to produce abundant color, distinctive flavor and delicate fragrance. Threads are the best form in which to purchase saffron as you can visibly see that there are no added ingredients.

Arroz Rojo

The red chile gives this rice dish amazing depth of flavor and color. It is virtually foolproof to prepare.

1	tbsp.	vegetable oil	15	mL
1½	cups	long-grain rice, uncooked	375	mL
1		medium onion, chopped	1	
3		garlic cloves, minced	3	
14	oz.	can crushed tomatoes	398	mL
1	tbsp.	red chile powder	15	mL
1¾	cups	water	425	mL
¾	cup	frozen baby peas, thawed	175	mL

In a medium saucepan, heat oil over medium-high heat. Add rice and sauté until evenly golden in color, about 7 minutes.

Add the onion and garlic and continue to sauté until onion is translucent. Stir in the tomatoes, chile powder and water; bring mixture to a boil. Reduce the heat to low; cover and simmer for 30 minutes, or until the liquid has been fully absorbed.

Remove from heat; stir in thawed peas; replace lid and allow to steam for an additional 15 minutes. Remove lid; fluff with a fork and serve.

Serves 8.

Rice

About half of the world's population includes rice as a diet staple. It has been cultivated for over 5,000 years. Long-grain rice is 3 to 5 times longer than wide. White or brown, it has less starch than medium or short-grained rice and the grains separate easily when cooked. Basmati, Jasmine, Texmati, Wehani and Louisiana Pecan are aromatic long-grain rice varieties with a nutty fragrance. Short grain (sticky) rice is almost round and has the highest starch content. It is used in Asian dishes from sushi to desserts. Medium grain rice is oval and has a soft texture. Italian Arborio rice is used for risotto and Valencia rice is traditional for Paella.

Clockwise from front lefthand side:

Pumpkin Bread with Cranberries, page 47
Cranberry-Orange Cream Cheese, page 48
Mexican Hot Chocolate, page 38

Raging Red Beans and Rice

1	lb.	dried red beans	500	g
2	tbsp.	vegetable oil	30	mL
2		large onions, chopped	2	
4		garlic cloves, minced	4	
1		medium red bell pepper, chopped	1	
1		medium green bell pepper, chopped	1	
2		celery stalks, chopped	2	
2		large tomatoes, chopped	2	
1	tsp.	ground cumin	5	mL
1	tsp.	ground coriander	5	mL
1½	tsp.	dried oregano	7	mL
½	tsp.	dried thyme	2	mL
1	tbsp.	red chile powder	15	mL
½	tsp.	cayenne pepper	2	mL
1	tsp.	crushed red pepper flakes	5	mL
2		bay leaves	2	
¼	cup	white vinegar	60	mL
1	tbsp.	hot sauce	15	mL
2	cups	long-grain rice, uncooked	500	mL

Soak, rinse and cook beans according to package directions.

In a large nonstick skillet, heat oil over medium heat. Add onion, garlic, peppers and celery and cook for 3 to 5 minutes, or until vegetables soften. Add tomatoes, cumin, coriander, oregano, thyme, chile powder, cayenne pepper, red pepper flakes, bay leaves, vinegar and hot sauce; cook for 15 to 20 minutes. Remove bay leaves. Add to beans and cook over medium heat until heated through, about 10 minutes.

Meanwhile, cook rice according to package directions.

To serve, place rice on a serving plate and spread the bean mixture on top.

Serves 6.

Risotto with Roasted Vegetables

Roasted vegetables add a rich intense flavor note to this superb risotto.

1		large red bell pepper	1	
$1\frac{1}{2}$	cups	frozen whole-kernel corn, thawed	375	mL
10-12		asparagus spears	10-12	
1	cup	water	250	mL
4	cups	vegetable stock	1	L
2	tbsp.	olive oil	30	mL
1		large onion, finely chopped	1	
3		green onions, finely chopped	3	
2		garlic cloves, minced	2	
2	cups	Arborio rice	500	mL
1	cup	dry white wine	250	mL
$\frac{1}{4}$	cup	grated Parmesan cheese	60	mL
1	tbsp.	chopped fresh parsley	15	mL
2	tsp.	dried oregano	10	mL
2	tsp.	dried thyme	10	mL

Preheat oven broiler.

Cut red pepper in half lengthwise and discard seeds and membranes. Place pepper halves, skin side up, on a foil-lined baking sheet. Sprinkle corn on baking sheet, and broil vegetables for 5 minutes. Add asparagus to baking sheet, and broil an additional 10 minutes, or until pepper is blackened. Be sure to stir corn and turn asparagus halfway through cooking time.

Place pepper in a plastic bag, seal and let stand for 15 minutes; then peel and chop pepper. Cut asparagus into ¼" (1 cm) pieces. Set roasted vegetables aside.

In a medium saucepan, bring water and vegetable stock to a simmer, but don't boil. Keep warm over low heat.

In a large saucepan over medium-high heat, heat oil. Add onion, green onions and garlic; sauté for 3 minutes. Add rice and cook for 2 minutes, stirring constantly. Stir in wine and cook for 5 minutes, or until liquid is nearly absorbed, stirring constantly. Add warm stock, 1 cup (250 mL) at a time, stirring constantly; between additions, cook until rice absorbs each quantity of stock before adding next stock quantity, about 20 minutes.

Stir in roasted vegetables, cheese, parsley, oregano and thyme. Cook an additional 2 minutes, stirring constantly.

Serves 8.

Risotto

Risotto is a rice dish that originated in northern Italy. Unlike most rice dishes, the technique of cooking risotto involves constantly stirring the rice in a simmering stock so that the liquid is slowly absorbed. Arborio rice is most commonly used, but another high-starch, short-grain rice may be substituted.

Measuring the Heat

In 1912, a pharmacist by the name of Wilbur Scoville developed a method to measure the heat level of chile peppers. The pungency is measured in multiples of 100 units from the bell pepper, which rates at zero, to the fire-breathing habañero, which measures in at the highest end of the scale at three hundred thousand. The units of measurement are referred to as "Scoville units" or "Scovilles" and are best described as units of dilution. A chile that rates 1 Scoville unit would take 1 unit of water to negate the heat. For example, it would take 30,000 to 50,000 units of water to neutralize a Tabasco pepper.

These days, many chile lovers use a new system which is referred to as the Official Chile Heat Scale, which rates the heat of chiles from zero to 10. On this simpler scale, bell peppers still rate as zero and habañeros rate at the top end of the scale with a 10. Comparatively, jalapeños rate as 5, serranos at 6 , and cayennes and Tabascos at 8.

It's interesting that regardless of the heat rating that a chile may have, everyone's palate is different and some lower registering chiles will taste hotter to some people than a higher registering chile. For example, an East Indian dish may taste very hot to someone used to Mexican spicing, even though the chiles used measure lower on the heat scale. Fortunately, most chile lovers are more concerned with flavor than with the heat measurement!

Preserves, Snacks, Salsas & Sauces

Chimichurri

Chimichurri originated in Argentina and is frequently served in Latin America as a condiment for grilled meats. Thanks, Chris, for introducing me to Chimichurri and for challenging me to create this recipe!

1/2	tsp.	ground cumin	2	mL
1/2	tsp.	red chile powder	2	mL
1/2	tsp.	dried oregano	2	mL
1/4	tsp.	crushed red pepper flakes	1	mL
1/4	tsp.	black pepper	1	mL
4		garlic cloves, peeled	4	
1	cup	fresh parsley	250	mL
2		green onions, coarsely chopped	2	
1		medium red bell pepper, coarsely chopped	1	
1/2	cup	olive oil	125	mL
3	tbsp.	red wine vinegar	45	mL

In a small nonstick skillet, add cumin, red chile powder, oregano, red pepper flakes and black pepper; toast over medium heat, stirring constantly, until fragrant but not browned. Remove from heat and set aside.

In food processor, pulse garlic until finely minced. Add parsley, green onions and red bell pepper; pulse until finely chopped.

Add toasted spices, olive oil and red wine vinegar and pulse in food processor until evenly mixed and a smooth paste forms.

Cover and refrigerate overnight. Mix well before serving.

Charred Pico De Gallo

8		Roma tomatoes	8	
1		medium onion	1	
3		jalapeño peppers	3	
3		garlic cloves, peeled	3	
1/4	cup	fresh cilantro leaves	60	mL
1/4	cup	fresh lime juice	60	mL

Preheat grill to medium-high heat.

Cut tomatoes and onion in half. Place on grill with cut sides down. Place jalapeños and garlic cloves on grill. Grill all sides of vegetables until charred.

In 2 batches, place roasted vegetables, cilantro and lime juice in food processor; chop to a chunky consistency.

Makes about 2 cups (500 mL).

Pictured on page 161.

Mexican Food Myth

Contrary to popular belief, original Mexican cocina (cuisine) was healthful and light. The Aztec diet was primarily vegetarian and was based on indigenous crops of corn, beans, chiles, tomatoes and squash (coastal regions also consumed fish and seafood). The heavy, fried Tex-Mex fare which people associate with Mexican cuisine is not at all representative of the diverse cuisines of Mexico.

Vegetables such as tomatillos, onions, chiles, garlic and tomatoes are often roasted and nuts, seeds, spices and herbs are often toasted to intensify flavors when used in traditional Mexican cuisine. Traditional cooking techniques include steaming food in cornhusks or other natural food wrappers, or grilling to enhance food flavors without adding additional fat.

Tomato Chutney

The similarities between cuisines of the world never cease to surprise me. This East Indian chutney, which is delicious served with the Chicken and Vegetable Curry featured on page 116, is very similar to Mexican and Latin American salsas. This chutney is not only simple and delicious, but very healthy as well!

2	tomatoes, chopped	2
1/4	onion, cut in slices and then quartered	1/4
2	jalapeño peppers or serrano chiles, finely chopped	2

Mix together all ingredients and add more heat (chiles) if desired.

Serves 4.

Roasted Chipotle Tomato Sauce

The smoky, rich flavor of the chipotle blends beautifully with the roasted tomatoes and onions in this recipe. Serve over your favorite pasta or on burritos and enchiladas.

2	lbs.	Roma tomatoes, cut in half lengthwise and ends trimmed	1	kg
1		large onion, cut in (1/2" or 1.3 cm) slices	1	
3		garlic cloves, peeled	3	
2		jalapeño peppers, cut in half lengthwise, ends trimmed and seeds removed	2	
1		lime, juice of	1	
3		chipotle chiles in adobo sauce or reconstituted dried chipotle chiles (see page 111 for instructions)	3	

Preheat oven to 500°F (260°C).

Arrange the tomatoes, onion slices, garlic and jalapeño peppers in a baking dish coated with nonstick cooking spray and bake for 35 minutes. Place roasted vegetables, lime juice and chipotle chiles in a food processor and process until mixture is smooth.

Sauce may be made ahead and reheated.

Makes 2 cups (500 mL).

Pictured on page 161.

Tomatillo Chipotle Salsa

This is a fast and deliciously simple salsa that will complement virtually any dish that you serve with it, particularly chicken dishes or quesadillas. The smoky heat of the chipotle complements the tangy flavor of the tomatillo, and it presents well whether served warm or cold.

1		dried chipotle chile	1	
½	cup	boiling water	125	mL
12		medium tomatillos	12	
1		medium white onion, cut in coarse chunks	1	
6		garlic cloves, peeled	6	

In a heavy skillet over medium heat, toast the chipotle chile for approximately 3 minutes, or until fragrant. Cool. Slit chipotle open with a knife and remove and discard seeds. Pour boiling water over chile in a small bowl and let soak for approximately 10 minutes.

Husk, rinse and pan-roast tomatillos, onion and garlic in a heavy skillet* over medium-high heat until brown and soft. Put chile mixture and remaining ingredients in a blender and process at high speed until the contents are almost liquid.

Makes about 2 to 2½ cups (500 to 625 mL).

*Note: Tomatillos, onion and garlic may be grilled or pan-roasted on a barbecue instead of cooking on the stove top.

Tomatillos

Tomatillos are surprisingly not members of the tomato family, but are actually members of the gooseberry family. They are available at Latin-American markets and some large supermarkets. They have a papery outer husk which should be removed, and then the tomatillos should be rinsed in soapy water, followed by clear water, to remove the sticky residue of the husks.

Oil of Olé

This oil is wonderful for stir-frying or anywhere you would use canola oil for cooking a savory recipe. It adds incredible flavor to any dish and can be put in small bottles for gift-giving.

12		dried hot red chiles	12	
2	cups	canola oil	500	mL
1½	tbsp.	cayenne pepper	22	mL
2	tbsp.	sesame oil	30	mL
		dried hot red chiles, for garnish		

Crush dried chiles and put them in a medium saucepan with the canola oil. Simmer over very low heat for 10 minutes, being very careful not to let the oil get too hot. Remove from heat and cool.

Stir in cayenne pepper and sesame oil. Cover pan and let sit at room temperature for at least 12 hours or overnight to develop flavors.

Place 3 dried chiles in each sterilized bottle that you will be using. Line a funnel with a double layer of cheesecloth and strain the oil into the sterilized bottles. Seal and label.

Makes 2 cups (500 mL).

Cold Infusion for Spiced Oil

Portuguese cooking uses "Piri-Piri" which is a simple combination of dried chili peppers and olive oil. In a sterilized 8 oz. (250 mL) jar, place ¼ cup (60 mL) of dried red chile peppers, crumbled. Fill the jar with extra virgin olive oil or a blend of canola and olive oil or straight canola. Seal and refrigerate for 1 month before using. Keeps, refrigerated, for another month.

Spicy Chile Vinegar

Try this vinegar with some olive oil in your next tossed green salad! It also makes a great hostess gift.

4	dried bay leaves	4
6	dried hot red chiles	6
4	garlic cloves, cut in half	4
	red wine vinegar	

Place bay leaves, chiles and garlic into a tall bottle. Fill the bottle with vinegar. Cork the bottle and let stand at least 3 weeks in a cool, dark place to allow the flavor to develop.

Green Chile Honey

Try this honey on biscuits, scones, bagels, muffins, pancakes or whatever else you can think of! The heat of the chile powders is a wonderful contrast to the sweet of the honey. Another great gift-giving idea!

2	tsp.	green chile powder	10	mL
1/2	tsp.	red chile powder	2	mL
1/2	cup	liquid honey	125	mL

In a small bowl, mix the chile powders into the honey. Store any surplus chile honey at room temperature.

Chile Notes

Chiles aid in the human body's process of digestion (some chiles seemingly help more than others!).

Margarita Jelly

This jelly will add color and flavor to any cheese and cracker tray. It also adds a delightfully different accent to muffins or toasted bagels.

1	cup	fresh lime juice	250	mL
1 1/4	cups	water	310	mL
1/2	cup	tequila	125	mL
1/4	cup	orange-flavored liqueur (Triple Sec, Cointreau or Grande Marnier)	60	mL
few	drops	green food coloring	few	drops
1/2	tsp.	unsalted butter	2	mL
4	cups	sugar	1	L
3	oz.	pouch liquid fruit pectin	90	g

Measure lime juice, water, tequila, liqueur, food coloring and butter into a large saucepan. Add sugar and mix well. Place saucepan over high heat and bring to a full, rolling boil, stirring constantly.

Immediately stir in liquid fruit pectin, making sure all pectin in pouch is used. Continue to stir and return to a full rolling boil. Boil hard for 1 minute. Remove from heat.

Pour quickly into warm, sterilized jars, filling to 1/4" (1 cm) from rim. Seal while hot with sterilized 2-piece lids.

Makes about 5 cups (1.25 L).

Piquant Pineapple Salsa

This salsa is incredible when served with ham! In additional to using this salsa as a condiment on the table, try it in your next sandwich.

14	oz.	can unsweetened pineapple tidbits, drained	398	mL
1/2		large red bell pepper, chopped	1/2	
3		green onions, thinly sliced	3	
2	tbsp.	white wine vinegar	30	mL
4-6	drops	jalapeño based hot pepper sauce	4-6	drops

Heat a large nonstick skillet over medium heat. Cook pineapple, red pepper and green onion 1 to 2 minutes, stirring constantly.

Add vinegar and hot pepper sauce; simmer for 1 minute. Add more hot pepper sauce, if desired, to taste. Cool. Cover and refrigerate up to 1 week.

Makes 1½ cups (375 mL).

Note: If fresh pineapple is available, this recipe is even tastier using half a large pineapple that has been peeled, cored and chopped.

Pictured on page 161.

Salsa– It's More Than a Dance Step!

Although most people think of salsas as being limited to the usual ingredients of tomatoes, onions, lime juice and jalapeño peppers, they can take on many other forms as well. And they don't even have to be hot! When you consider that "salsa" is the Spanish word for sauce, whether cooked or uncooked, a whole world of possibilities unfolds.

Salsas are wonderful complements to light cooking as they are low in fat and calories and give foods a great kick. What really makes salsa "get up and dance" is the use of fresh ingredients that range from mangoes, papaya, pineapple, cranberries, peaches to onions, tomatoes and corn. Salsas are served alongside or atop any number of foods – use your imagination and have some fun with them! You can start practicing your salsa steps right now with the salsa recipes featured in the Preserves, Snacks, Salsas & Sauces section of this book.

Cranberry Orange Salsa

This salsa is wonderful with roasted turkey or grilled chicken.

1		jalapeño pepper	1	
½	cup	fresh cilantro leaves	125	mL
2		green onions, cut in chunks	2	
12	oz.	fresh cranberries, rinsed	341	mL
3		navel oranges, peeled and sectioned	3	
½	cup	liquid honey	125	mL

Cut stem end off jalapeño pepper and add to food processor with washed cilantro. Pulse until finely chopped. Remove from food processor and place in a medium-sized bowl. Add green onions and cranberries to food processor and pulse until coarsely chopped. Add to the jalapeño and cilantro mixture in bowl. Pulse orange sections in food processor until coarsely chopped. Add oranges to the cranberry mixture and stir in liquid honey. Stir well to combine, cover and refrigerate for several hours or overnight to allow flavors to blend.

Makes about 2 cups (500 mL).

Another serving suggestion: To serve as an appetizer, spread a teaspoon of light cream cheese on a cracker, top each cracker with a teaspoon of Cranberry Orange Salsa and garnish with cilantro sprigs.

Pictured on page 161.

Sweet Heat

This combination of sweet and heat is delightful. Not exactly low calorie, but a really special treat for the holiday season or for gift giving!

½	cup	chopped pecans	125	mL
1	cup	unsalted butter	250	mL
1	cup	sugar	250	mL
4	tsp.	red chile powder	20	mL
2	tbsp.	water	30	mL
1	tbsp.	light corn syrup	15	mL

Toast pecans in a nonstick skillet over medium heat until lightly browned. Butter a 9 x 13" (23 x 33 cm) baking pan and sprinkle the nuts over the bottom.

Over low heat, melt the butter in a medium-sized heavy saucepan. Whisk in the sugar and chile powder and cook over medium-low heat until the mixture comes to a full rolling boil, stirring constantly. Stir in the water and corn syrup and continue cooking and stirring until the mixture reaches 290°F (143°C) (it is critical to use a candy thermometer to ensure the correct temperature is reached).

Pour the mixture into the prepared pan and quickly spread it evenly over the nuts. Refrigerate until set. Break the candy into bite-sized pieces and store in a covered container.

Variation: For a really decadent treat, melt ¼ lb. (125 g) of semisweet chocolate in a double boiler and spread over the candy after it has cooled while in the pan. Refrigerate until set. As above, break the candy into bite-sized pieces and store in a covered container.

Baked Tortilla Chips

Tortillas are the fastest growing portion of the baking industry in North America. They are being used in everything from tostados, quesadillas, burritos, enchiladas to wraps. Try baking your own tortilla chips, using this recipe, for healthier results and better flavor.

2	tsp.	canola oil	10	mL
12		corn tortillas	12	
1/4	tsp.	salt (optional)	1	mL

Preheat oven to 425°F (200°C).

Brush oil lightly over 1 side of each corn tortilla. Sprinkle with salt, if desired. Cut each tortilla into 8 or 10 wedges and arrange in a single layer on 2 baking sheets that have been lightly oiled or coated with a nonstick cooking spray. Bake each batch 4 minutes, rotate baking sheets in the oven, and continue baking for 4 to 6 minutes or until chips are crisp. Let cool.

Makes 8 dozen chips.

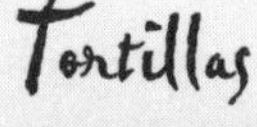

Tortillas

Unleavened flatbreads, tortillas are the everyday bread of Mexico and have become very popular throughout North America. Handshaped and baked on a griddle, tortillas are made with wheat flour or cornflour (masa harina).

Preserves, Snacks, Salsas & Sauces

Clockwise from front lefthand side:

Piquant Pineapple Salsa, page 157
Charred Pico de Gallo, page 151
Tomatillo Chipotle Salsa, page 153
Cranberry Orange Salsa, page 158

Spicy Cornmeal Crisps

These little snacks are delightfully different and low in fat. Add more chile powder to them if you prefer them spicier.

1/2	cup	cornmeal	125	mL
1 1/2	tsp.	ground red, green or chipotle chile powder	7	mL
1/4	tsp.	black pepper	1	mL
1	tbsp.	butter or margarine	15	mL
1/2	cup	boiling water	125	mL

Preheat oven to 400°F (200°C). Lightly oil or coat 2 baking sheets with nonstick cooking spray.

In a small bowl, combine cornmeal, chile powder and black pepper. Add butter or margarine and, using a pastry cutter, cut into the cornmeal mixture until it resembles fine crumbs. Add boiling water and stir well.

Transfer the cornmeal mixture into a plastic sandwich bag and cut a 1/4" (1 cm) hole in 1 corner. Pipe the mixture into 4" (10 cm) strips on each baking sheet, leaving approximately 1" (2.5 cm) between strips. Bake, 1 sheet at a time, for about 10 minutes, or until crisp and golden.

Makes lots!

Hot and Healthy

Eating a teaspoon (5 mL) of pure chile powder for the vitamin A (60 milligrams) and eating an ounce (30 g) of fresh chiles for the vitamin C (5,000 international units) will meet your daily recommended requirements.

Savory Popcorn Seasoning

Packages of this seasoning mix are a great gift-giving idea. Lots of flavor without any calories and quantities can be easily multiplied to make larger batches.

2	tsp.	red, green or chipotle chile powder	10	mL
2	tsp.	dried basil	10	mL
1	tsp.	ground cumin	5	mL
1	tsp.	ground coriander	5	mL
½	tsp.	ground oregano	2	mL
½	tsp.	salt (optional)	2	mL

Combine chile powder, basil, cumin, coriander and oregano. Toast in a nonstick skillet over medium heat until fragrant but not browned. Remove from heat; cool and add salt, if desired.

Store in a jar and shake over hot popcorn.

Makes enough seasoning for 2 batches of popcorn.

Popcorn

Popcorn probably originated in Mexico. Samples have been found that are over 5,000 years old, but it had made its way to China and India even before Columbus discovered America. The first use of wild corn and cultivated corn was popping. 1,000-year-old grains of popcorn have been found in Peru, and they still pop. Talk about shelf life! Popular in North America from the late 1800s on, Americans today eat over 60 quarts each per year. Native American folklore told of spirits that lived in the popcorn kernels. When their houses were heated they got angry and finally exploded from their homes in a burst of steam. Each popcorn kernel has a drop of water within a circle of soft starch, surrounded by a hard shell. The water expands as the kernel heats up, increasing pressure against the shell. Finally the shell explodes.

Chocolate Chile Pretzels

These are absolutely addictive – don't turn your back because they'll disappear quickly! They make great gifts for friends and family at Christmas.

2	cups	semisweet chocolate chips	500	mL
1	tsp.	cayenne pepper	5	mL
1	tsp.	vegetable oil	5	mL
36-48		large pretzels	36-48	

In a double boiler over medium heat, add chocolate chips and cook until chocolate is melted; stirring frequently. Add cayenne pepper and vegetable oil; stir until smooth and well combined.

Dip pretzels in the chocolate mixture 1 at a time. You may wish to dip only 3/4 of the pretzel, for effect, or coat the entire surface, depending on your preference. Place coated pretzels on waxed paper and refrigerate until hardened.

Makes 3 to 4 dozen.

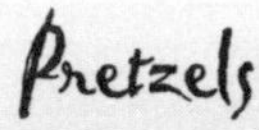

Pretzels

From Roman times people have enjoyed these baked treats. Originally soft and chewy, today we also have the choice of crisp crunchy pretzel sticks and twisted knots. The knot shape was developed in the early 600s, but the first pretzel factory wasn't established until 1861, in Pennsylvania. The soft, chewy pretzels are often sold hot by street vendors and spread with mustard.

Radiant Rub

Instead of using a traditional marinade or sauce, why not try a low-fat alternative that promises to "light" up your next serving of beef, chicken, pork, fish or seafood.

2	tbsp.	grated Parmesan cheese	30	mL
1	tbsp.	coarsely ground or cracked black pepper	15	mL
1	tbsp.	red, green or chipotle chile powder	15	mL
2	tsp.	dried basil	10	mL
2	tsp.	dried rosemary	10	mL
2	tsp.	dried thyme	10	mL
½	tsp.	garlic powder	2	mL

Combine all ingredients in a small, nonstick skillet and toast (see page 112 for instructions). Remove spices from skillet and transfer to an airtight container in a cool, dry place.

Makes just over ⅓ cup (75 mL).

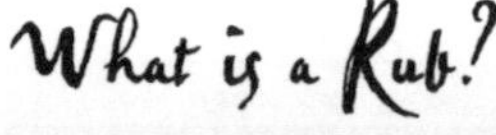

What is a Rub?

Rubs are dry mixtures of spices and herbs that can be kept indefinitely in an airtight container and stored in a cool, dry place. A general rule would be to use 3 tbsp. (45 mL) to cover 1 lb. (500 g) of food. When using rubs, make sure that they are applied to food that is completely dry. To apply a rub, place the food item that you are coating and the appropriate amount of rub mixture in a zip-top bag and shake until thoroughly coated. Roast, grill or sauté the coated foods until food reaches desired doneness.

Desserts

Watermelon Margarita Granita

This dessert can be made well ahead of serving, is fresh and light with incredible flavor. Plus, your guests will love the presentation!

1		small seedless watermelon, cut in chunks	1	
2		limes, juice of, 2 to 4 tbsp. (30 to 60 mL)	2	
3	tbsp.	sugar	45	mL
1/4	cup	tequila	60	mL
3	tbsp.	orange-flavored liqueur (Triple Sec, Cointreau or Grand Marnier)	45	mL
18		frozen green seedless grapes (see instructions below)	18	

Place all ingredients, except grapes, in a blender and process until smooth. Pour mixture into a 9 x 13" (23 x 33 cm) pan; cover and place in freezer.

Periodically remove pan from freezer and scrape with a fork to make the mixture light and fluffy.

Place 6 margarita or sorbet glasses in freezer for at least 30 minutes to chill. Remove from freezer and fill with granita just before serving. Garnish with 3 frozen grapes per glass.

Serves 6.

Frozen Grapes

Frozen grapes are a breeze to make and a real conversation piece. Rinse grapes and drain well. Make sure that the grapes are fairly dry. Place grapes on a plate or in a bowl and freeze. After 2 hours, the grapes are ready to eat. Any uneaten grapes can be stored in the freezer in a plastic bag to be enjoyed later.

Strawberry Margarita Mousse

Light and delicious, this dessert is perfect to "extinguish the fire" that you ignited for that special dinner party. The best part is that you're able to make it hours before your guests arrive.

5	cups	whole strawberries, washed and hulled	1.25	L
3/4	cup	sugar	175	mL
2		envelopes unflavored gelatin (2 tbsp. or 30 mL)	2	
3	tbsp.	boiling water	45	mL
1/4	cup	tequila	60	mL
2	tbsp.	orange-flavored liqueur (Triple Sec, Cointreau or Grand Marnier)	30	mL
2	cups	fat-free plain yogurt	500	mL

Place strawberries and sugar in a blender; process until smooth. Transfer strawberry purée to a large bowl.

In a small bowl, combine gelatin and boiling water. Stir constantly for 5 minutes, or until gelatin dissolves.

Add tequila and orange-flavored liqueur to the strawberry mixture; mix well. Stir in the gelatin mixture. Cover and chill for 15 minutes, or until the mixture begins to thicken.

Add the yogurt and stir until well blended. Pour the strawberry mixture into 6 margarita glasses; cover and chill for at least 4 hours, or until set.

Serves 6.

Cantaloupe Dessert Soup

Cantaloupe is loaded with beta carotene and vitamin C. It's hard to believe that anything that tastes so sweet and fresh could be so good for you!

2		large cantaloupes, cut in chunks	2	
½	cup	orange juice	125	mL
1		fresh lime, juice of	1	
2	tbsp.	fresh mint	30	mL
1	tbsp.	liquid honey	15	mL
1	cup	vanilla low-fat yogurt	250	mL
		mint sprigs, for garnish		

Place half of the cantaloupe in a blender and add orange juice, lime juice, mint and honey; process until smooth. Add remaining cantaloupe; process until smooth.

In a large bowl, combine cantaloupe mixture with yogurt and mix well. Cover and chill until ready to serve. Garnish each serving with a mint sprig.

Serves 6.

Cantaloupes

North American cantaloupes are muskmelons, not true cantaloupes, which are grown only in Europe. More complex in flavor and with a more dense flesh than watermelons, cantaloupes are ripe when they seem heavy for their size, they are slightly softened at the blossom end and the aroma is fruity and sweet. Refrigerate ripe cantaloupes, and wrap in plastic to avoid their absorbing other food odors if storing for more than 2 days. Cantaloupes are high in vitamins A and C.

La Fresa Sorpresa

"La Fresa Sorpresa" or Strawberry Surprise is an unusual combination of ingredients that blend to create an incredible taste sensation.

6	cups	sliced strawberries	1.5	L
1/4	cup	tequila	60	mL
1/2	cup	orange juice	125	mL
2	tbsp.	orange-flavored liqueur (such as Triple Sec, Cointreau or Grand Marnier)	30	mL
1	tbsp.	balsamic vinegar	15	mL
2	tsp.	freshly ground black pepper	10	mL
		orange slices, for garnish		

In a large bowl, combine strawberries, tequila, orange juice, orange-flavored liqueur, balsamic vinegar and black pepper. Cover and refrigerate for 4 hours or overnight, stirring occasionally. Garnish with orange slices, if desired.

Serves 6.

Shortcut Slicing:

To quickly slice mushrooms, strawberries or kiwis, try using an egg slicer, preferably with stainless steel wires for strength.

Grilled Fruit Kebabs

Why not prepare your dessert on the barbecue? Fresh summer fruits are delicious "hot" off the grill with this buttery cinnamon baste. This is a refreshingly different and unique ending to a barbecued summer meal. Feel free to try any number of fruit combinations for a fabulous taste experience.

1/4	cup	melted butter	60	mL
2	tbsp.	brown sugar	30	mL
1		fresh lime, finely grated rind and juice of	1	
1	tsp.	cinnamon	5	mL
4		1" (2.5 cm) slices fresh pineapple, peeled, cored and cut in 1" (2.5 cm) pieces	4	
4		apples or pears, cored and cut in 1" (2.5 cm) pieces	4	
4		nectarines or peaches, pitted and cut in 1" (2.5 cm) pieces	4	
1/2		honeydew melon or cantaloupe, peeled, seeded and cut in 1" (2.5 cm) pieces	1/2	
2		bananas, peeled and cut in 1" (2.5 cm) pieces	2	

Spray barbecue grill with nonstick cooking spray and preheat barbecue to medium-high.

In a small bowl, stir together melted butter, brown sugar, grated lime rind, lime juice and cinnamon until sugar is dissolved.

Thread fruit alternately onto each of 8 skewers. Brush kebabs with butter mixture and place on barbecue grill. Grill for 6 to 8 minutes, turning frequently and brushing generously with butter mixture, until the fruit starts to brown and is heated through.

Serves 8.

Pears in Red Wine

This elegant dessert can be made be made hours ahead of your dinner party so that you can relax and enjoy your guests. For a delightful variation, try substituting fresh sliced peaches in place of pears.

1/4	cup	sugar	60	mL
1		orange, washed and cut into 1/4" (1 cm) slices	1	
2		lemons, washed and cut into 1/4" (1 cm) slices	2	
1/4	tsp.	ground cardamom	1	mL
8		whole cloves	8	
4		black peppercorns	4	
1		5" (13 cm) cinnamon stick	1	
26	oz.	bottle dry red wine	750	mL
6	cups	fresh pears, peeled and sliced	1.5	L

Combine sugar, orange, lemons, cardamom, cloves, peppercorns, cinnamon stick and red wine in a large saucepan. Bring to a boil over medium-high heat and cook for 15 minutes. Remove from heat and cool to room temperature.

Strain wine mixture through a colander or sieve over a bowl; discard solids. Combine wine mixture and pears in a medium nonmetal bowl; cover and chill for at least 4 hours, stirring occasionally.

Serves 6.

Grown in tropical rain forests, and a member of the ginger family, the most intense cardamom flavor is from the green (not white) pods. Grind the pods with a spice or coffee grinder or with a mortar and pestle. you can sift out the shell or add it to soups and stews where it will be absorbed into the liquid. Cardamom is prized by East Indian and Scandinavian cooks. The aroma is a blend of ginger, coriander, pepper and nutmeg. The flavor is sweet and spicy. Coriander may be used as an alternative.

Decadent Strawberry Nachos

A truly decadent dessert treat!

3	cups	sliced fresh strawberries (see page 171 for a shortcut method to slice)	750	mL
1/4	cup	sugar	60	mL
1/4	cup	almond-flavored liqueur (such as Amaretto)	60	mL
3/4	cup	fat-free sour cream	175	mL
2	tbsp.	sugar	30	mL
1/4	tsp.	cinnamon	1	mL
6		6" (15 cm) flour tortillas	6	
2	tbsp.	melted butter	30	mL
2	tsp.	sugar	10	mL
1/4	tsp.	cinnamon	1	mL
2	tbsp.	sliced almonds, toasted	30	mL
1	tbsp.	shaved semisweet chocolate	15	mL

Combine strawberries, 1/4 cup (60 mL) sugar and almond-flavored liqueur in a bowl; stir well. Cover and refrigerate for at least 1 hour to allow flavors to blend.

Combine sour cream, 2 tbsp. (30 mL) sugar and 1/4 tsp. (1 mL) cinnamon in a small bowl; stir well. Cover and refrigerate.

Preheat oven to 400°F (200°C). Using a pastry brush, lightly brush 1 side of the tortillas with melted butter. Cut each tortilla into 6 wedges and arrange on 2 ungreased baking sheets. Sprinkle tortilla wedges evenly with 2 tsp. (10 mL) sugar and 1/4 tsp. (1 mL) cinnamon. Bake for 6 to 8 minutes, or until crisp. Remove from oven and cool.

Drain strawberries and reserve liquid for another use (like sipping while you prepare this dessert!).

Place 6 tortilla wedges on each of 6 dessert plates. Top each tortilla wedge with strawberries and a dollop of sour cream mixture. Sprinkle toasted almonds and shaved chocolate evenly among nachos.

Serves 6.

Caramel Banana Tortillas

The combination of bananas and caramel sauce (or rum!) always remind me of the Caribbean.

4		10" (25 cm) flour tortillas	4	
6		ripe bananas, sliced	6	
6	tbsp.	firmly packed brown sugar	90	mL
2	tsp.	cinnamon	10	mL
1/4	cup	melted butter or margarine	60	mL
2/3	cup	whipping cream	150	mL
1/4	cup	sugar	60	mL
1	tsp.	vanilla extract	5	mL
1/2	cup	fat-free sour cream	125	mL

Preheat oven to 350°F (180°C).

Place 2 tortillas on each of 2 ungreased baking sheets. Top with bananas. Combine brown sugar and cinnamon; sprinkle evenly over bananas. Drizzle tortillas with melted butter. Bake for 10 minutes.

Meanwhile, beat whipping cream with sugar and vanilla extract until stiff peaks form. Stir in sour cream.

When tortillas are cooked, cut each tortilla into quarters. Arrange 2 quarters on each dessert plate and top with sauce.

Serves 8.

Mexican Chocolate Truffle Tart with Sinful Sauce

This is definitely not a light dessert, but I'm a firm believer that all good (or great) things can be enjoyed occasionally and in moderation. This is truly a special dessert for a very special celebration!

Chocolate Cinnamon Crust:

1 2/3	cups	all-purpose flour	400	mL
3/4	cup	powdered sugar	175	mL
1/3	cup	unsweetened cocoa powder	75	mL
1	tsp.	vanilla extract	5	mL
1	tsp.	ground cinnamon	5	mL
1	cup	unsalted butter	250	mL

Chocolate Truffle Filling:

1	lb.	semisweet chocolate, cut into chunks	500	g
1/2	cup	unsalted butter, plus 2 tbsp. (30 mL)	125	mL
1	cup	sugar	250	mL
4		eggs, lightly beaten	4	
1	tsp.	vanilla extract	5	mL
2	tsp.	instant coffee granules	10	mL

Sinful Sauce:

1/4	cup	unsweetened cocoa powder	60	mL
1/2	tsp.	cornstarch	2	mL
1/2	tsp.	ground cinnamon	2	mL
1/2	cup	fresh orange juice	125	mL
1	tsp.	grated orange zest	5	mL
1	cup	chocolate syrup	250	mL
		whipped cream, for garnish		
		ground cinnamon, for garnish		

Preheat oven to 350°F (180°C).

To prepare crust, place flour, powdered sugar, cocoa powder, vanilla and cinnamon in a food processor. While processing, add butter in small amounts until dough forms on top of the blade. Remove dough from food processor and press into a well-greased 10" (25 cm) flan or spring form pan. Bake for 10 minutes, or until dough is set. Remove from oven to cool.

Mexican Chocolate Truffle Tart

with Sinful Sauce continued

To make filling, place chocolate and butter in a metal bowl over simmering water and stir until melted completely. Remove from heat, add sugar, eggs, vanilla and instant coffee granules; mix well. Pour into prepared crust and bake for 45 minutes, or until the filling is set.

To prepare sauce, stir together cocoa powder, cornstarch and cinnamon in a small saucepan. Whisk in orange juice and zest and stir over medium-high heat until thickened. Add chocolate syrup (Hershey's works well) and stir until the sauce is heated through.

When the Truffle Tart is cooked, cool for 20 minutes. Cut the tart and serve topped with warm Sinful Sauce, whipped cream and a sprinkle of cinnamon for garnish.

Serves 12.

Pictured on page 179.

Chocolate Truffles

Named after the rare savory fungus prized by gourmets, chocolate truffles are rich blends of melted chocolate, butter or cream, sugar and flavoring such as coffee, nuts, liqueurs, spices, etc.

Sherried Pine Nut Yogurt

My husband, Jim, makes the most wonderful sherry. This wonderfully simple dessert incorporates the delightful combination of toasted pine nuts and his amazing sherry.

2	tbsp.	pine nuts	30	mL
3	tbsp.	sherry	45	mL
2	cups	vanilla low-fat frozen yogurt, softened	500	mL

In a small nonstick skillet, toast pine nuts over medium heat until they are lightly browned. Remove from heat and cool.

Stir pine nuts and sherry into yogurt until mixture is well combined and has a smooth consistency. Serve immediately.

Serves 4.

Pine Nuts

Pine nuts, which are also called piñons or Indian nuts, are found inside pine cones which must be heated in order to remove the nuts. This intensive harvesting process is what makes them so expensive and special. Fortunately, the flavor of pine nuts is so assertive, you need to use very few of them in order to enjoy their distinctive taste.

Pine nuts are rich in fat and can turn rancid quickly. Try storing them in an airtight container in the refrigerator (for up to a month) or in the freezer (for up to 6 months) to keep them fresh. Unfortunately, chilling pine nuts will soften the texture, but that is easily remedied by toasting them as described in the recipe above. Toasting pine nuts not only restores crispness, but enhances their unique flavor.

Desserts

Mexican Chocolate Truffle with Sinful Sauce, page 176

Jenny's Pavlova

There's absolutely nothing fiery about this recipe! I wanted to include it, however, because it's become very "hot" with my parents. Our dear friends, Sal and Lorne Lindstrom, moved back from Australia several years ago. With them, they brought this delightful dessert recipe, named after Russian ballerina Anna Pavlova, that Sal obtained from her dear friend Jenny. Jenny, your gift has been enjoyed by many, across the continents! Thank you.

Meringue:

3		egg whites	3	
1½	cups	berry sugar	375	mL
1	tsp.	white vinegar	5	mL
1	tsp.	cornstarch	5	mL
½	tsp.	vanilla	2	mL
¼	cup	boiling water	60	mL

Fruit 'n' Cream Topping:

1	cup	whipping cream	250	mL
		sliced strawberries, for garnish		
		sliced kiwis, for garnish		

In a large bowl, combine all meringue ingredients and beat with an electric mixer on high speed until stiff peaks form, about 5 to 8 minutes.

Spoon meringue mixture onto a baking sheet covered with a sheet of aluminum foil. Spread meringue evenly in a circle approximately 8" (20 cm) across and 1" (2.5 cm) deep.

Turn oven on to 350°F (180°C) (do not preheat oven), place meringue in oven and bake for 30 minutes. Reduce heat to 250°F (120°C) and continue baking for an additional 30 minutes. Turn oven off and leave meringue in oven until oven is cold.

When ready to serve, beat whipping cream until stiff. Spread over meringue and decorate with sliced strawberries and kiwis.

Serves 8.

Green Chile Chocolate Chip Cookies

Every once in a while you've got to splurge and have something really decadent. These cookies certainly "fire" up your enthusiasm for a special treat!

1	cup	unsalted butter or margarine, softened	250	mL
1	cup	firmly packed light brown sugar	250	mL
1/2	cup	granulated sugar	125	mL
2		eggs, lightly beaten	2	
2	tsp.	vanilla extract	10	mL
2 1/2	cups	unbleached white flour	625	mL
3	tbsp.	green chile powder	45	mL
1/2	tsp.	baking powder	2	mL
1/2	tsp.	baking soda	2	mL
1 1/2	cups	semisweet chocolate chips	375	mL

Preheat oven to 350°F (180°C).

In a large mixing bowl, cream the butter, sugars, eggs and vanilla with an electric mixer until light and fluffy.

In another bowl, mix together the flour, green chile powder, baking powder and baking soda. Gradually add the flour mixture to creamed mixture and beat until completely combined and smooth. Add the chocolate chips and mix until just combined.

Drop the batter by heaping teaspoonfuls (7 mL) onto baking sheets coated with nonstick cooking spray. Bake for approximately 10 minutes, or until lightly browned. Remove from oven and place cookies on wire racks to cool.

Makes 3 dozen cookies.

Chile-Cherry Bread Pudding

with Cherry Sauce

Thanks, Sheri, for sharing this delicious bread pudding recipe.

Chile Cherry Bread Pudding:

2/3	cup	dried cherries	150	mL
1/4	cup	tequila	60	mL
1		loaf French bread, cut into 1/2" (1.3 cm) cubes	1	
14	oz.	can unsweetened applesauce	398	mL
1 1/2	cups	evaporated skim milk	375	mL
2/3	cup	sugar	150	mL
2		eggs, lightly beaten	2	
1/2	tsp.	ground cinnamon	2	mL
1/4	tsp.	ground nutmeg	1	mL
1	tsp.	red chile powder	5	mL
2/3	cup	chopped pecans	150	mL
1/2	cup	pine nuts	125	mL

Cherry Sauce:

16	oz.	frozen cherries, thawed	500	g
1/4	cup	powdered sugar	60	mL
1/4	cup	kirsch or cherry-flavored brandy	60	mL
		vanilla low-fat frozen yogurt or vanilla low-fat ice cream, if desired		

Combine cherries and tequila in a small bowl and marinate for at least 1 hour. Drain cherries and reserve tequila (you probably need something to sip on while you finish this recipe!).

Preheat oven to 350°F (180°C). Thoroughly spray a 9 x 13" (23 x 33 cm) baking dish with cooking spray and evenly spread the bread over the bottom. In a large bowl, combine the applesauce, milk, sugar, eggs, cinnamon, nutmeg and chile powder; whisk to blend. Sprinkle the cherries, pecans and pine nuts over bread in pan. Pour applesauce mixture over bread, cherry and nut mixture in pan. Cover the pan with aluminum foil and bake for approximately 1 hour, or until the center of the pudding is firm.

While pudding is baking, make sauce by adding thawed frozen cherries, powdered sugar and kirsch to blender; purée until smooth.

Remove pudding from oven and cool slightly. Spoon pudding into bowls over frozen yogurt or ice cream, if desired. Top with cherry sauce.

Serves 6.

Apple, Cranberry and Red Chile Crisp

The appearance and color of this dessert is almost as good as the flavor!

Spiced Brown Sugar Oat Topping:

2/3	cup	flour	150	mL
2/3	cup	firmly packed brown sugar	150	mL
2/3	cup	old-fashioned rolled oats	150	mL
1/2	tsp.	ground cinnamon	2	mL
1/4	tsp.	ground nutmeg	1	mL
1/2	cup	margarine or butter, cut into pieces	125	mL

Apple, Cranberry and Red Chile Filling:

1/2	cup	sugar	125	mL
2	tbsp.	flour	30	mL
1	tbsp.	red chile powder	15	mL
1/2	tsp.	ground cinnamon	2	mL
1/4	tsp.	ground nutmeg	1	mL
8		apples, peeled, cored and cut into eighths	8	
1	cup	fresh frozen cranberries	250	mL

Preheat oven to 350°F (180°C).

To make topping, in a medium bowl, combine flour, brown sugar, rolled oats, cinnamon and nutmeg. Cut in butter, using a pastry blender, until mixture is well blended and resembles fine crumbs. Set aside.

To make filling, in a large bowl, combine sugar, flour, chile powder, cinnamon and nutmeg. Add apples and cranberries, stirring to thoroughly coat fruit and prevent apples from turning brown. Transfer fruit mixture to a 9 x 13" (23 x 33 cm) baking dish that has been coated with nonstick cooking spray. Sprinkle the topping over the fruit mixture and bake for about 1 hour, or until the apples are very tender and the topping is crisp and brown. Serve warm.

Serves 6 to 8.

The MJM Grande Publishing Company Ltd. is pleased to introduce their new Spice Line!

The new spice line features pure ground medium red, green and red chipotle chile powders and offers a truly unique taste experience. The spices are organically grown, packaged and privately labeled for The MJM Grande Publishing Company Ltd. in Velarde, New Mexico and are available in two-ounce packages.

Pure Ground Medium Red Chile Powder

Red chiles have been eaten in the Americas for hundreds of years – in fact, Christopher Columbus wrote about them in his diaries and said that " . . . the people won't eat without it, for they find it very wholesome." Red chiles are dried and hung on "ristras" ("ristras" look like bananas hanging on a tree), or are ground into powder.
Price – $4.95 per two-ounce package.

Pure Ground Medium Green Chile Powder

A green chile is an unripened chile, which will eventually turn red, orange or purple, depending on the variety. Fresh green chiles are only available for a few months each summer, usually starting in late July. Green chiles have a wonderful flavor that is perhaps best experienced when they are roasted (especially over an open flame) and then peeled, or else ground as a powder. Green chile cuisine has been developed in New Mexico and is only about a century old. Try some green chile powder today!
Price – $6.95 per two-ounce package

Pure Ground Medium Red Chipotle Powder

Chipotle chiles are ripened jalapeños that have been smoke-dried over peat. Chipotles are extremely hot and have a fabulously hot, fruity-smoky flavor. For years a favorite in Mexico, this chile has taken the North American gastronomic world by storm. Chipotle is featured in everything including sauces, soups, salads, seasoning pastes, breads, etc. Experience the unforgettable flavor of chipotle soon!
Price – $6.95 per two-ounce package

See the Order Forms on pages 193 and 195 for more information on how to place your order today!

Also available from The MGM Grande Publishing Company Ltd.

the Fire 'n' Ice cookbook

Mexican Food with a Bold New Attitude

by Linda Matthie-Jacobs and Sheri Morrish

- A national best seller with international acclaim
- Featured in Hemispheres, the United Airlines in-flight magazine
- Bold flavors perfect for everyday meals and entertaining
- Beautifully illustrated with colorful, enticing photographs
- Low-fat, low-salt without compromising flavor
- Designed to lay flat

The Fire 'n' Ice Cookbook is a fabulous fiesta of flavors inspired by contemporary and traditional Mexican cuisine. It's a lusty tribute to people with a passion for exciting new food experiences. This creative collection of recipes offers a wide variety of foods that satisfy, from fiery to mild and from sophisticated to simple. You'll appreciate this innovative and delicious approach to fun food and enlivened eating. The Fire 'n' Ice Cookbook will delight you with its beautiful photographs and east-to-follow recipes. Enjoy the tantalizing tastes of "Mexican food with a bold new attitude"!

Original Edition
ISBN: 1-895292-40-9
6" x 9" Quality Paperback with Coil Binding
143 Pages, 8 Color Photographs
Price: $14.95

Revised Edition (to be available early in 1999)
ISBN: 1-894202-54-6
7" x 10" Quality Paperback with Otabind-Style Binding
196 Pages, 10 Color Photographs
Price: $15.95 U.S. and $18.95 CDN

The Fire 'n' Ice Cookbook

"What a fun book. Being a native Texan, I can appreciate it fully!"
– Sally Bernstein, Editor In Chief, Sally's Place

"I love spicy foods and found this cookbook a delight!"
– The Cookbook Collector, Zachary, Louisiana

"Another exceptional thing about this book is its eight stunning photographs. The props and background are chosen with a distinct eye . . . "
– Chile Pepper Magazine, Fort Worth, Texas

"There are so many delights to be sampled and savored, again and again . . . "
– Wisconsin Bookwatch, Oregon, Wisconsin

"I thoroughly enjoyed your cookbook . . . "
– Patricia Sharpe, Senior Editor, TexasMonthly

"The colorful cover shows hot peppers submerged in ice that will instantly draw you in. Anyone who would like to add some spice to everyday dinner fare will enjoy this well-designed book."
– Books for Cooks, Quick 'n Easy Magazine

"I've enjoyed reading the recipes and looking at all the photographs. Now I look forward to trying some of the recipes".
– Anne Lindsay, Internationally Acclaimed Cookbook Author

"And what about that cover – I would have to say it is one of THE BEST that I have seen in a very long time."
– Bill Granger, Book Promotion, Inc.

"You'll appreciate this innovative approach to food and eating."
– The International Cookbook Revue, Madrid, Spain

"Here is another one of those great surprises: a seemingly unassuming little cookbook with a great big punch."
– Cinnamon Hearts, Modesto, California

"Combined with the health benefits of capcaisin and chiles, the recipes in "The Fire 'n' Ice Cookbook" are fabulously healthy, nutritious and delicious!"
– The Cookbook Collector's Exchange, San José, California

"A passionate tribute to fiery foods, The Fire "n" Ice Cookbook is an easy-to-read, easy-to-make collection of contemporary and traditional Mexican recipes."
– Daily Press, Victorville, California

"If you prefer your ethnic foods authentic . . . even when this sometimes means fiery . . . this cookbook is for you."
– The Sanford Herald, Sanford, North Carolina

Order Form

Telephone orders:
Call toll free: 1-888-MJM-FIRE and have your AMEX or VISA card ready

On-line:
Orders, information about our complete product line or sign up for our biannual e-mail newsletter entitled "Fireworks": mjmgrand@cadvision.com or visit our website located at http://www.cookingwithfire.com

Cooking with Fire

Postal orders:
Please make check or money order payable to:
The MJM Grande Publishing Company Ltd., P.O. Box 4031, Station C, Calgary, Alberta, Canada, T2T 5M9

Light the Fire – Fiery Food with a Light New Attitude!
____ x 15.95 U.S (18.95 CDN) = $______

The Fire 'n' Ice Cookbook – Mexican Food with a Bold New Attitude (Original Edition – While Quantities Last)
____ x 14.95 U.S (14.95 CDN) = $______

The Fire 'n' Ice Cookbook – Mexican Food with a Bold New Attitude (Revised Edition – To be Available Early 1999)
____ x 15.95 U.S (18.95 CDN) = $______

Pure Ground Medium Red Chile Powder - 2 oz. package
____ x 4.95 U.S (5.95 CDN) = $______

Pure Ground Medium Green Chile Powder - 2 oz. package
____ x 6.95 U.S (8.95 CDN) = $______

Pure Ground Medium Red Chipotle Chile Powder - 2 oz. package
____ x 6.95 U.S (8.95 CDN) = $______

Shipping:
$4.00 for the first book (or book equivalent) and
$2.00 for each additional book (or book equivalent)
- There is no additional charge for shipping spices when ordered with books = $______

Subtotal = $______
Sales tax in Canada add applicable GST (7%) or HST = $______
Total order = $______

Payment: ❍ Check or Credit card: ❍ AMEX or ❍ VISA

Card number: ______________________ Expiry date: ____/____

Name on card: ______________________

U.S. and international orders are payable in U.S. funds.

Name: ______________________

Street: ______________________

City: ______________________ Prov./State ______________

Country: ______________________ Postal Code/Zip: ______________

For fund raising or volume purchases, contact The MJM Grande Publishing Company Ltd. for volume discount rates.

Order Form

Telephone orders:
Call toll free: 1-888-MJM-FIRE and have your AMEX or VISA card ready

On-line:
Orders, information about our complete product line or sign up for our biannual e-mail newsletter entitled "Fireworks":
mjmgrand@cadvision.com or visit our website located at
http://www.cookingwithfire.com

Cooking Fire

Postal orders:
Please make check or money order payable to:
The MJM Grande Publishing Company Ltd., P.O. Box 4031,
Station C, Calgary, Alberta, Canada, T2T 5M9

Light the Fire – Fiery Food with a Light New Attitude!
____ x 15.95 U.S (18.95 CDN) = $______

The Fire 'n' Ice Cookbook – Mexican Food with a Bold New Attitude
(Original Edition – While Quantities Last)
____ x 14.95 U.S (14.95 CDN) = $______

The Fire 'n' Ice Cookbook – Mexican Food with a Bold New Attitude
(Revised Edition – To be Available Early 1999)
____ x 15.95 U.S (18.95 CDN) = $______

Pure Ground Medium Red Chile Powder - 2 oz. package
____ x 4.95 U.S (5.95 CDN) = $______

Pure Ground Medium Green Chile Powder - 2 oz. package
____ x 6.95 U.S (8.95 CDN) = $______

Pure Ground Medium Red Chipotle Chile Powder - 2 oz. package
____ x 6.95 U.S (8.95 CDN) = $______

Shipping:
$4.00 for the first book (or book equivalent) and
$2.00 for each additional book (or book equivalent)
- There is no additional charge for shipping spices
when ordered with books = $______

Subtotal = $______
Sales tax in Canada add applicable GST (7%) or HST = $______
Total order = $______

Payment: ❍ Check or Credit card: ❍ AMEX or ❍ VISA
Card number: ______________________ Expiry date: ____/____
Name on card: ______________________

U.S. and international orders are payable in U.S. funds.

Name: ______________________
Street: ______________________
City: ______________________ Prov./State ______________________
Country: ______________________ Postal Code/Zip: ______________________

For fund raising or volume purchases, contact The MJM Grande Publishing Company Ltd. for volume discount rates.